HIGH
IMPACT
BUSINESS
PRESENTATIONS

HIGH IMPACT BUSINESS PRESENTATIONS

The secrets behind the success of the world's most persuasive speakers

Lee Bowman

with Andrew Crofts

C

CENTURY
BUSINESS

This paperback edition was first published in Great Britain in
1993 by
Century Business
An imprint of Random House UK Ltd
20 Vauxhall Bridge Road, London SW1V 2SA

Random House Australia (Pty) Ltd
20 Alfred Street, Milsons Point,
Sydney, NSW 2061, Australia

Random House New Zealand Ltd
18 Poland Road, Glenfield,
Auckland 10, New Zealand

Random House South Africa (Pty) Ltd
PO Box 337, Bergvlei, South Africa

Hardback published 1991

Printed and bound in Great Britain by
Mackays of Chatham PLC, Chatham, Kent

A catalogue record for this book is available from the British
Library

ISBN 0–7126–56251 (p)

For *La Susie!*

Acknowledgements

Naturally I am greatly indebted to my late father for his original work in spoken communications and for providing the foundation for what has been a fascinating career.

In the book I mention various colleagues who continue to contribute not only to the success of Kingstree, but also to the evolution of our service to clients. I would, however, like to acknowledge here the special contribution of my fellow director, Nigel Brown, who runs our UK practice, and of his right hand man, John Walter.

It also goes without saying that none of us would be able to maintain the frenetic pace without the support and encouragement of our administrative and financial teams.

This would clearly be the place to acknowledge the excellent help I received from Andrew Crofts, in putting the book together. Andrew was able to get a firm grasp of the Kingstree approach, and he had the ability to articulate the key points in a tight, concise way. His help has been invaluable.

Contents

Introduction

Although The Kingstree Group is based in London, our work crosses the Atlantic, and our methods are used by some of the world's most senior people.

When he was US Secretary of Defence, Caspar Weinberger was due to make a speech at a major maritime conference at the Kennedy Centre in Washington, when a senior member of the Saudi royal family died. President Reagan asked Weinberger to represent him at the funeral and someone else had to be found to make the speech for him the following day.

The task was given to John Lehman who was then US Navy Secretary and has now gone into the business world. He had been trained by Kingstree.

When Lehman's speech-writer, a young naval commander, looked at Weinberger's draft he realized that it was a good speech for Secretary Weinberger but quite unsuited to Lehman's more direct style and personality. The speech-writer took Weinberger's draft away to re-work it overnight.

The following morning a driver picked up the speech-writer on his way to collect Lehman and take him to the Kennedy Centre, where he would be speaking alongside others like the Vice President. When Lehman got into the car the speech-writer was still working on the tail-end of the speech, and he handed the beginning of it across to the Navy

Secretary. As he began to read Lehman found himself feeling carsick, and had to put the speech down until they got there.

'Boy,' he said to the speech-writer, 'I hope that Bowman guy knows what he's doing or we're all in trouble.'

Half an hour later he went up onto the podium and gave the speech to a standing ovation. No-one knew that he was reading; no-one knew that it was the first time he had ever seen the words; everyone thought he was working from a few notes. The Kingstree system worked for him, just as it has for hundreds of other important speakers.

The point of this story is that it is perfectly possible for everyone who has been through the right training to be able to deliver a script, word for word, and for the audience to believe that the speaker is working from notes. Their delivery will be relaxed and confident, and the speaker will invest the message with his knowledge of and commitment to the subject.

By investing the message with the appropriate emphasis it has been brought to life. This has the added advantage of making it easier for the audience to follow what is being said, and remember it.

The only limit which a script will impose on a speaker is the need to have a lectern or something similar on which to place the actual papers. Apart from that, there is very little difference between using notes and full scripts for the skilled and trained presenter.

A radical alternative to traditional presentation training

We believe that most of the traditional advice on how to speak and present in any given situation is out of date, and in many respects it is actually WRONG.

We believe that most traditional advice actually makes people worse at communicating. It makes them more nervous. It makes them more boring. It makes them less attractive to the audience, and it makes their messages less clear and less memorable.

Our method of working, which has proved successful with all the thousands of clients that we have worked with, is based on the concept that people communicate best when they are being themselves, not when they are following a set of 'rules' laid down by someone who has never met them.

The Kingstree system

There are two levels to the work we do with our clients. At one level we teach them a *system* which will allow them to stand up in front of an audience and read a script while appearing to speak spontaneously.

Even if they have never seen the words before they will be able to give the audience the impression that they are entirely familiar with the subject matter.

At the same time they will be able to give the impression that they are not reading, but merely working from notes and thinking up what they are saying as they go along.

They will also be able to impress the audience with their eloquence and power as speakers, making what they say interesting to listen to and memorable.

The system involves a physical, mechanical 'technique' which, once learnt, will help anyone to deliver all his or her spoken communications more confidently and effectively.

It is the Kingstree system which the US Navy Secretary was using when he delivered Caspar Weinberger's speech, and it is a system which is used by many of the most powerful and influential people in the worlds of big business, politics and diplomacy who are our clients.

It can work for anyone.

The system for delivering words from a text, however, is only a small part of the overall Kingstree approach.

The Kingstree approach

Our *approach* to spoken communications encompasses a much broader and more complex set of philosophies regarding how people communicate with one another, and why spoken communication works so well for some people and so badly for others.

We believe that everyone who stands up to speak needs to achieve three things.

They need to:

- PROJECT THEIR PERSONALITY
- KEEP THE AUDIENCE'S ATTENTION

• MAKE THEIR KEY MESSAGES MEMORABLE

These goals may sound glaringly obvious, but very few people actually consider them when planning to give a presentation, or know how to achieve them successfully.

Most people stumble from one situation to the next, doing the best they can to get by, and never really achieving their potential.

Perhaps they have never stopped to consider just what is going on in the minds of their listeners, or perhaps they are so nervous they can't control what they are saying, or perhaps they are so enthusiastic about their subject they don't realize that other people need to have it 'sold' to them.

Whatever the reason, most people are very poor communicators when they stand up to speak.

We have discovered, however, that by employing a consistent 'approach' to the problem of spoken communications, which starts with the planning of what is to be said, and continues through the writing of the speech, the staging of the event and the final delivery of the words, anyone can make himself a hundred times more effective as a speaker.

From formal speeches to informal presentations

Most people don't actually stop to think about how to communicate until they are asked to make a formal speech or presentation in front of an important or large audience.

Yet all of us are using the medium of spoken communication all day long.

Every day we all talk to other people one to one, or in casual meetings. Some of us have to brief subordinates, while others have to report to the boss. Some days we have to go to job interviews or we are required to train a group of people. We might need to sell something or to raise money. . . the number of situations in which we need to use spoken communications is virtually endless.

In all these situations it is important to have some strong presentation techniques to help us get our messages across, and to give us confidence that we can do it consistently.

What this book will teach you

In this book we describe the Kingstree system and the approach. We will explain to you exactly why it is that some people are so effective when they speak and show you how you can achieve the same results.

We will look at all the most important situations where you are likely to need to explain, persuade or unfluence, whether it is one person or several thousand.

If you can master these basic concepts, and then practise them, we guarantee that:

- You will be able to improve your communication performance in almost every area of your life
- You will gain confidence at work and in your personal life
- You will be able to control the nerves which beset every speaker
- You will be able to cut down the time needed to prepare for any spoken communication from a formal speech to an informal meeting
- You will be able to project your real personality effectively
- You will demonstrate that you can handle more responsibility and bigger jobs
- You will be able to sell yourself, your company, your products or your services far more successfully
- You will bring yourself to the attention of the people who matter
- You will be able to persuade others to do things your way
- You will be able to increase your earning power
- You will be able to make what you say memorable

How it All Started

Learning from the President

My father, Lee Bowman Senior, was a Hollywood actor and businessman. He was also highly active in Republican party politics.

He was walking in New York one day in the 60s. As he passed a television shop he noticed President Lyndon Johnson making a speech on the multiple screens flickering in the window. The impact of what Johnson was saying and how he was saying it was multiplied by the number of times his image was repeated in the display. My father stopped to watch.

He had met Johnson through his political activities and, even though he didn't agree with him politically, he felt that he was the kind of man we needed to be President at the time – basically a tough, plain-talking, hard man from Texas – which was what Johnson was.

At that stage television was still a pretty new medium for the politicians, and as my father watched the President perform, he realized that the man had been advised badly. He had been told to come across to the audience as an apologetic, grandfatherly figure, which bore no relation whatsoever to his true personality.

The results were blatantly false and phoney. Because of the number of screens the insincerity was reduplicated from every angle.

The broadcast made a considerable impact on my father, and the more he thought about it the more he came to the conclusion that if the President himself was receiving such bad advice on television presentation, the chances were that the same thing was happening within his own political party in Washington.

He decided to devise a programme to train his colleagues in how to avoid the problems that the President had created for himself by trying to change his image and to teach them how to put their true personalities across.

Looking for the secrets of success

At that stage my father could not quite see what the secret of success was, but he set out to find it. All he knew was that there had been a style change in the President's delivery and that it was bad news because it created a distraction from the important message which he was trying to put across.

He went to Washington and set up a programme for the Republican National Committee and began to analyse in depth what was wrong with communication on television and why it was wrong.

Although he started by seeing the problem as it applied to television, he soon realized that the same principles could work in any situation where someone was communicating with others through the spoken word, trying to put across messages, trying to persuade. It might be a huge political rally involving audiences of thousands, or it might be a one-to-one meeting where it was crucial to make an impact and change someone's mind fast.

My father became convinced that there must be one basic approach which would cover all these situations, one secret which, once learnt, would lead people to be able to persuade others more effectively.

Twenty-five years later we are still researching the subject and finding out new things about the ways in which people can persuade and influence one another through the spoken word.

Moving into the business world

Two or three years after my father started the Washington programme, the Bethlehem Steel Company heard about what he was doing for the Republican leadership, including President Nixon's cabinet, and thought that its own senior company officers could use the same type of advice.

My father flew out to Bethlehem for a meeting with the patrician chairman of the company and his president. After explaining his approach, my father asked them if they had ever done anything like it before. The two men exchanged glances and confessed. For the previous six months they had been taking the company 'plane up to

New York to meet an opera singer on Central Park South, who had been giving them 'breathing exercises' among other things.

My father thought for a few moments. 'Gentlemen,' he said, 'you look about the same age as me, around 50, is that right?' They agreed that was about right. 'Well, it looks to me as if you have been doing a pretty good job of sucking in air for some considerable number of years without any help, but if you two think you need to go up to New York for breathing exercises I'm not your guy.' He stood up to leave, but he had made his point and the contract was his.

Traditional wrong advice

The point of the story is that the advice from the opera singer was typical of the sort of irrelevant information about presentation techniques which, to this day, has been part of the presentation training scene. In reality the only thing that matters is whether the people listening to you can remember what you have said and have come away with the right impression of you.

Traditional training companies will tell you how to stand, how to gesticulate, how to breathe, how to look at people, how to talk.

They will put you in a strait-jacket of techniques which will make you look and sound just like everyone else they have trained. In everyday life you have no trouble with any of these skills, and the combinations in which you use them make up your personality. If you abandon everything natural to you, and substitute all these 'acquired' mannerisms, you will appear unnatural and uncomfortable.

Learning the 'confidence' trick

The reason that people feel they need to learn the traditional 'skills' is because the nervous tension which attacks most people when they stand up to speak in a formal setting destroys their confidence in themselves and makes them distrust their own natural powers of communication and persuasion.

If a trainer can help someone to overcome the confidence problem with techniques on how to put a message across effectively, and can show how to overcome the nervous tension with other techniques, then the speaker is left free to be him or herself.

By royal appointment

My father's system developed and word spread of its effectiveness, though he did little to promote it himself. He was even invited to advise members of a European royal family on how to make speeches and present themselves during state visits.

A convert to the cause

At the time this was all happening I had only the haziest idea of what it was my father was up to. I knew he was teaching people how to speak better, and to me that seemed a pretty extraordinary thing for people to be willing to pay for.

I was working very successfully as an investment banker on Wall Street for Reynolds Securities, after starting with W E Hutton and then E F Hutton. I had a broad exposure to different aspects of the financial world, and my major skill seemed to be as a sales manager.

After being sent out to California as Regional Sales Manager, I was called upon to give a talk on the Bond Market and syndication of debt issues.

Although I had never taken any real interest in what my father was doing, I rang him and asked if he thought he could help me with this speech.

He told me to rent some video equipment and have it sent out to the house in Beverly Hills, and he would show me what he did for his clients.

I arrived at the house with no idea what to expect, and my father went through the same routine he did with all his clients. By the end of the session I was astonished by what I had seen of my own style.

When he asked me to give my speech to the cameras I was horrified to see how I behaved. Just like Johnson, I was putting on an act in the speech – my 'act' being influenced by my perception of how the smart young Wall Street banker should talk – which was entirely foreign to my natural style.

I realized that the approach which he had worked out was completely revolutionary because it allowed people to speak to even the most important audiences in the same natural, relaxed way they communicated every day. I saw immediately that it should be turned into something much bigger than the few contracts which my father had been given around the country.

A major part of my job at that time was to take senior company officers around to talk to the investment community about new offerings of securities and shares. Without realizing it I had witnessed exactly the same problem with all of them: their personalities changed when speaking, as I saw in myself and as my *father had seen in the window of that television shop. Suddenly I could see a way of solving their problems.*

I became very excited by the whole concept, and I felt certain that it could be developed into a major business.

My father was quite happy for me to do whatever I wanted with the idea, so I put my money into going out to sell the system to major corporations, and worked with my father as an apprentice to learn all the tricks which he had perfected so far.

Spreading the word

I had two reasons for believing that my father's approach should be made more widespread.

The first was that it seemed a completely valid system to me, and I thought more people should know about it.

Secondly, the atmosphere in America at that time was very left-wing, with the system of free enterprise under eloquent attack on a number of fronts. There were anti-Vietnam protests, racial tensions leading to major riots and a number of vociferous anti-business lobbies.

I felt that the leaders of the free enterprise system needed to express its case more effectively. Business leaders were frequently bad at putting across the emotional issues of the need for business prosperity in order to create a healthy economy and society. In my opinion, the major corporations were doing nothing to articulate that view, and I believed that was largely because they did not know how to put simple messages across effectively, eloquently and persuasively.

I believed that my father's approach would give great credibility to the business leaders of the time in putting their views across to the world outside their own corporate walls. As a side effect I believed it would also help them to communicate better amongst themselves, with all the improvements which that would mean for their productivity, creativity and quality of life.

We went out with a marketing campaign, but it took us six months to win the first account.

The problem was that we were spending most of our time trying to educate people about why they should consider the scheme at all, never mind why we were qualified to handle it for them. The reaction from most of the companies we approached was that their senior people didn't need help in communicating. After all, if they weren't good communicators they wouldn't have got to the top.

Our arguments remained consistent; the perspective from which we were approaching the subject of spoken presentations assumed that our clients were already effective, persuasive communicators. By reaching their eminent positions they had demonstrated that they could communicate their ideas consistently, and they had the right personality characteristics to compel clients, colleagues and industry peers to hire, trust and promote them against stiff competition.

But their effectiveness, we argued, as persuasive communicators had primarily been proven in an informal, small meeting environment.

Our approach was to prove to them how and why they were effective communicators in a relaxed conversational setting, and then give them the skills and the confidence to approach the most daunting presentation assignments in their own conversational style.

If they followed our methods, our clients would come across as relaxed and confident with whatever material they were delivering, and no matter how difficult the circumstances of the presentation, even if they were actually under enormous stress.

The people listening to them would get accurate impressions of their real personalities, and would also easily be able to retain the key points in their messages.

We were completely opposed to the view that there was any one 'style' which should be adopted for making effective presentations. We disagreed entirely with our competitors' 'sausage machine' approach, which suggests that there can be a list of 'do's and don'ts' for making presentations. The challenge, as we saw it, was to discover what put each client at ease in high-stress environments, and then encourage the client to employ his or her own innate communications style consistently.

We were aiming to eliminate the apparent change in personality which occurs with so many presenters who have been schooled in traditional rigid guidelines. We wanted clients to 'be themselves' under the most difficult circumstances, proving that their own individual style is always the most effective style of communication for anyone, and is universally reassuring to audiences.

The big clients begin to arrive

By the end of the first six months my money was running out. I was about to give up and go back to the banking world, when Standard Oil of Ohio, which is now part of BP, Alcoa, the biggest aluminium producer in the world, and Kaiser Industries, a heavy industrial group, gave me contracts to work with their senior executives.

Having set up those initial contracts with my father doing the training, I then met a senior man from Teledyne, a major high-technology conglomerate in California, who was about to take all his senior people from Los Angeles around the country to meet the heads of the 125 or so companies which the group owned, few of whom had ever seen them before.

By that stage I had been understudying my father for a year and he agreed that I was now able to take on the training myself. From that moment the clients just kept coming, and we started to hire colleagues and teach them how to deliver our consulting services.

Moving into Europe

By the late 70s our biggest customer was Gulf Oil. They had a problem in London which they asked me to handle, so I came over in 1982 and stayed at Claridges Hotel.

While in London I decided to make some sales calls, following up introductions from existing North American clients and doing some cold calling. As a result we began advising the most senior executives of the National Westminster Bank, Phoenix Assurance, Pearsons and several other major companies.

As the contracts built up I began coming to England one week a month. That became two weeks a month, and it was about to become three weeks when Morgan Bank gave us a major contract to expand our programme to London, Paris and Frankfurt.

I decided it was time to hire someone to open a permanent European office when I met my wife Sue in London. She is English and since she already had two children in school it was obvious which of us was going to have to move! So I set up a branch office of The Kingstree Group in London, continuing to handle work on both sides of the Atlantic. I began by doing the European work myself, while simultaneously recruiting and training the best people I could find. Sue began to work for the firm, learning how to master everything from word processing to helping to manage our finances and advising on recruitment. She remains a director today. All this was while doing a superb job as mother of the two children we have added to her older two. In 1982 Kingstree Group (UK) Ltd was organized with an investment by a number of our consulting clients.

Today Kingstree works for the biggest companies in every sector of industry and commerce. In most cases we can only work for one brand leader at a time in each field because of the need for discretion and confidentiality. If we are privy to presentations which top executives are going to make in the future, either to internal or external audiences, they have to be sure that they can trust our discretion completely.

Normally our introduction to a company is at the top. We will start by training the chairman, chief executive or finance director. Once they are happy with the Kingstree approach and can see how effectively it works for them, those initial clients then recommend us to their fellow directors and managers.

The basic principles are identical whoever the client is and whatever the audience is going to be. We just have to tailor the client's actual message to fit the particular event or meeting.

World leaders

At the time of writing this book we have worked for 12 of the top 50 companies in the world. We have worked for four out of the top ten UK companies and seven of the top ten US ones. We have worked for 18 of the world's top 100 banks, three of the top five petroleum companies and three of the top five aerospace companies. We have also worked with the global leaders in the chemical, computing, office equipment, electronics, food, forest products, mining, motor-vehicle manufacturing and scientific and photographic sectors.

What follows are the secrets which we impart to these clients.

Part I:
The Approach – How it Works

· 1 ·

Why is Spoken Communication Important?

Successful people take the art of spoken communication very seriously indeed. An American company, for instance, which had recently appointed a new president felt that he needed help with his presentation skills. The president was agreeable to working with us, but said that he wanted to meet me first.

As a result I had to take Concorde from London to New York, connect with a flight to Chicago, get a car and drive to the company's office. I then talked to the president for 12 minutes – which was enough time to convince him we were the people for the job – before getting back into the car and heading for the airport. Within 24 hours of setting out I was back in my house in London.

That is how seriously some people take this business.

Everyone from the chairman of a company right down to the most junior manager needs to be able to communicate verbally. They have to be able to talk to their bosses, their subordinates and their colleagues. They have to talk to customers and suppliers, investors and informal meetings.

The ones who succeed are the ones who can get their messages across clearly and memorably, and can project their personalities.

Companies are being asked to perform publicly in an increasing number and variety of situations such as 'beauty contests' (a term used to describe competitive pitches for new business, and when raising finance).

Professional people such as accountants and lawyers who have traditionally maintained low profiles are now finding that they have to compete for business. Highly trained information technology specialists, who often find expressing themselves difficult, are now striving to win big contracts. The fate of whole companies can hang on the ability of an executive to put over key points persuasively.

All spoken communication is selling

All spoken communication is selling in one way or another. It may not be a product that you are selling, it may just be a point of view or an idea, but often the most powerful way to put it across is with the spoken word – not the written word.

What do you remember?

If you look back over your life you will be able to remember many of the things said to you, whether by your parents, friends, spouses, bosses or subordinates.

You will not often be able to remember things that you have read with anything like as much clarity.

You won't, of course, be able to remember the exact words that were said to you in most cases, but you will remember the 'essence', which means you will have retained the message which the speaker wanted you to understand.

The written word has many other powers, and in many cases is a far more time-efficient way of transferring information, particularly if it is lengthy or detailed; but the written word rarely has the ability to 'make a difference' in such a succinct and powerful way. Most people can remember quotes from Churchill, Lincoln and many other great communicators, but very few would be able to quote anything which these people committed to paper.

The Bible is full of stories and parables told by one generation to the next before anyone actually wrote them down.

The spoken word is more powerful than the written

Yet the common belief is the opposite. Over the last few centuries the written word has reigned supreme as the most respected form of communication.

All western education has been based on written communication in the form of books. Even when someone goes to a university lecture the first thing he or she does is get out a paper and pencil and start writing notes. Instead of listening to and digesting the spoken words of our teachers, we all try to get them down in note form so that we can review them later and then use them in an exam, which is usually also in a written format.

A professor will make written notes (sometimes having gleaned the information from other people's books) and will deliver them to people who are also writing them down and who will frequently repeat them later in an essay or exam paper.

So in an academic setting the whole communication process is heavily weighted towards the visual and literary. Yet if you hear people quoting something that they remember from college days, it will usually be something their professor 'said', and they will not have to refer to their notes in order to remember the message; it will be firmly implanted in their brains.

However, much of the information they have learnt through traditional study will be lost to them the moment they come out of the examination room.

A revolution in the way we communicate

In the late twentieth century, with the arrival of widespread visual and audio communications media like television and telecommunications, that tradition is finally changing. People are now realizing the power and strategic importance of the spoken word.

Senior managers now realize that in order to run their companies effectively they have to come out of their offices and communicate directly with their people, just as great generals like Field Marshal Montgomery have to leave their tents on the battlefield and talk to their troops, and great politicians have to get out onto the streets (or at least into the television studio) and tell people what it is that they want to achieve.

Spoken communication has been a concern of all modern politicians. From the time of Churchill, who worked very hard on his radio broadcasts and personal speeches, to today, there has been an awareness amongst all of them of the power of spoken communications. President Reagan and President Mikhail Gorbachev both achieved positions of international leadership through their ability as communicators.

Business leaders have paid lip-service to the importance of the subject, but haven't really done much about it until very recently. Even though they are beginning to focus on it as a problem, only very few of them have recognized that it is a strategic problem, which has a major influence on how their businesses perform.

Wasting money by wasting words

Often companies spend enormous sums of money gathering large numbers of people together at conferences and meetings, only to hear spoken messages which simply aren't sticking in the minds of the audiences. Every day in offices around the world millions of man-hours are wasted in meetings which drag on too long without achieving any results, just because they aren't being run correctly and the anticipated communication fails to occur.

Who knows how many people fail to reach their full potential simply because they are not able to communicate their ideas and abilities to the right people, or how many contracts and orders go to the wrong companies, because the right companies weren't able to sell themselves effectively?

Most senior executives know they need to do something about the effectiveness of spoken communication, if their major initiatives on subjects like quality and productivity are going to be sold effectively to their employees. But few business people know what to do to achieve any noticeable improvement in presentation standards.

Every presentation and every meeting provide opportunities for effective communication, but most of them are wasted.

Far too many business people still believe that if they have something really important to communicate to a target group they should put it in writing.

Yet if they stopped to think about their own reading habits they would realize just how few written messages aimed at them actually get read at all. And of those that are read, most are skimmed through and rarely remembered.

Take 'control' of the communication

If you write something down for somebody, he or she then has the choice of reading it or not. You have no way of reinforcing the message, or of adjusting the emphasis of the second sentence to match the reactions to the opening words.

You probably won't even be in the room when it is read, and even if you are it is unlikely you will be able to judge how the reader is reacting to your words.

If you are speaking, however, you can gauge from the response whether or not you are getting through, and you can adjust your message and your delivery accordingly.

If you can see that the person has understood the point that you are making, then you can move on. If he or she obviously hasn't then you can repeat it or put it another way. You can slow down, speed up or go back over something you think needs stressing. In a word, you have 'control' over the communication.

If you are the chairman of a company, for instance, you might need to convince people that they have to change the ways they work. You will not be able to convey the urgency of the change on paper.

Only by talking to them, convincingly, can you convey that changes in their behaviour are critical to the survival of the company. The depth of your commitment will be difficult, if not impossible to judge unless they hear you talk about it convincingly.

The same principle goes through every level of every company, and is relevant every time anyone opens his mouth to speak. The key points have always got to come through, even if you are only speaking to one person. Your depth of knowledge on the subject you are talking about must be readily apparent, as must your conviction, integrity and all the things that make up your personality.

Spoken communication is a strategic issue

Many major companies are beginning to realize that the effectiveness of their spoken communications is really a strategic issue, something which has to be addressed at the highest levels of management before it can work at every other level.

One large office products company, for instance, has in the last few years instigated a quality initiative which illustrates this point.

We became involved because the firm's European operation decided it wanted to hold a meeting in Brussels, to bring together all the top managers of all the European country operations. It wanted them to hear presentations from a New York director, the executive in charge of the quality initiative in Europe and a number of other executives from around the world. The subject was how the quality initiative would positively influence the company's results.

The communication problem was that a quality initiative is actually an abstraction. The concept of quality is itself something which is very hard to make solid and identifiable. And these abstractions had to be 'sold' to an audience by a group of executives who were largely unknown to them.

The danger was that it would seem like just one more 'good idea' with no meat or substance to it, and the message would seem to have no relevance to the recipients.

The challenge that we faced was to look at what they were proposing to accomplish, get together with all the people who were going to be participating in this three-day meeting, and convince them that the only way they were going to sell the quality approach was if the recipients believed that the speakers were committed to it. The recipients also had to believe that they were listening to people of sound judgement who wouldn't be pushing an initiative that didn't make sense.

Unless they were able to couch each element of the initiative in terms that the recipients could immediately identify with, and relate to their own business objectives, the speakers would fail to convince anyone.

It seems obvious when stated like that, but we discovered when we looked at each of the various segments of the conference, which were being produced in different countries, that they were completely unco-ordinated and had no central theme.

We had to find a way of pulling the whole thing together. We started with the senior executive in Europe. We had to make absolutely sure that his opening statement followed all our guidelines. He had to show everyone in the room exactly what the quality initiative would do for them.

Once we had got his presentation right, that gave us a backbone on which our clients could build the rest of their conference.

We then looked at each subsequent presentation, and by working with each of the individuals involved, we were able to take a disjointed, apparently unco-ordinated effort and put it together in such a way that it made absolute sense to the participants. Everybody could relate personally to the quality initiative because every conceptual point was illustrated by a concrete example or case study. The result was that everyone in the audience got behind the initiative and had a clear enough picture of it to be able to sell it on to the other people in their home countries.

We came across another classic case when we were called in to see a major supplier to the aviation industry. It was selling a product which in some cases cost as much as a whole aircraft.

One way this company sells its products is to invite the airline buying teams to visit its headquarters for two or three days. The buyers are given a series of briefings from various members of the company, ranging from board directors to technical experts.

We discovered that the potential buyers brought with them a range of people; someone from operations, someone from finance, someone from the flight department; and other individuals, all of whom had different backgrounds and different objectives.

We noticed that the selling company would receive questions on day two of the visit, concerning subjects which they had covered on day one. The questions in many cases would not have been necessary had the presentations on day one been effective, because the questioners were mostly asking for clarification or re-statement of messages that should have come across clearly the first time.

On further examination we found that there was no central control of the presentation process.

Although it was decided in advance who would talk to the buying groups, there was virtually no co-ordination between the various segments which were being put together to present the company's case.

There was no system that would allow anybody to vet the whole presentation in order to check that it was consistent, or to ensure that everyone was promoting the same competitive advantages.

The recipients from the airlines needed to understand and remember what the company was telling them, but we could see that the variety of messages and styles which they were being subjected to made that difficult.

The various presenters would each prepare material in isolation, turn up at the appointed time and talk to the audience, having no idea what the audience had heard from the previous speaker or what they would be hearing from the next one. There was no central control of visual aid material, or of presentation training or of the main selling messages, all of which should have been consistent throughout.

The buyers needed to be given confidence that if they bought this particular product for many millions of pounds, they would be dealing with a unified team of people who had a sufficient depth of knowledge and consistency of approach to understand the airline's particular problem and to provide support. They weren't being given that confidence.

We examined the whole system and made a series of recommendations as to how it could be done better. Out of that came a cogent approach which ensured that when customers came to visit they received a coherent message.

We wanted to make sure that each segment was capable of standing on its own, but equally that it fitted into a mosaic. So that at the end of two or three days it was very easy for customers to walk away knowing what they had learnt on the visit, and what the advantages to them would be of buying from that company. In other words they knew with great certainty what the competitive advantages of that company's products were over its rivals.

KEY POINTS

- Spoken communication is a strategic issue
- Spoken communication can be more effective than written communication in the majority of cases
- Effective speakers can 'take control' of a communication
- Tradition dictates that spoken communications are governed by the rules of written communication – this is entirely wrong!
- Ineffective spoken communications waste money on a massive scale

· 2 ·

What's Different About This Approach?

When you ask for advice from friends or colleagues on what to do when you have to make an important presentation, they always say things like; 'oh, just be natural' or 'just be yourself, you'll be fine'.

It sounds easy, but of course when you actually stand up to do it, with the adrenalin rushing, your memory a blank and your mouth parched, it is the hardest thing in the world to do.

We have defined what it actually means to 'be yourself', and have developed a system which will allow you to achieve it every time, virtually without thinking about it.

Over the last 25 years my colleagues at Kingstree and I have analysed exactly how normal conversational communication works, particularly when used by the powerful figures of the business and political worlds.

We believe that if you can understand how normal, informal spoken communication works, then you will be able to understand what you must do and keep doing for your formal spoken communications to work for you.

All the traditional views and advice of how presentations should be made, whether it be a formal speech, a sales pitch, an internal company meeting or an after-dinner speech, are based on a literary frame of reference.

In other words they are based on the rules of grammar, syntax, structure and language that apply to written communication. There is also a belief that a presenter has to meet certain arbitrary standards to achieve excellence.

In our view the standards are wrong.

We believe that normal, casual conversation is the most effective form of spoken communication

When you are sitting in a relaxed situation with friends or colleagues, talking naturally, the chances are that you are listening to what everyone else is saying and they are listening to you.

When you don't understand something, you show it in your face, or you ask a direct question. When you do understand what you are being told, you demonstrate it with a small nod or a word of encouragement, which tells the other person it is safe to continue talking because you have understood what's been said so far.

They are doing the same to you, listening, understanding and then either indicating that they need to know more or that they now have the necessary information.

You need to recognize, then capture this normal style of communication and make it work for you on demand in any given situation.

Some of the traditional advice

Someone who is nervous about speaking in public is often keen to be given some 'golden rules' about what should or shouldn't be done. We all want certainties to cling to when we are entering uncharted waters. There is no shortage of people willing to offer advice on the subject – some of it patently ludicrous.

They all talk, for instance, about the problems involved with breathing. Sometimes they talk about these problems at great length.

One piece of advice given to readers by an eminent writer on the subject starts by suggesting that they breathe through the nose, 'counting slowly to four, and then stop. Hold the breath for a further count of four and then release it gently through the mouth'.

He goes on to suggest that with the next breath you extend the count to six and so on up to 16, although he does warn against the dangers of over-oxygenation resulting in dizziness. The section ends with the advice 'if you are prone to sniffing, blow your nose before you step up.'

Blow your nose? If we were asked to take on a client who did not yet know how to keep his nostrils clean, I think I would suggest that he was not yet quite ready to appear in public.

If you do have a problem with a dripping nose, would it not be feasible to blow it discreetly in front of the audience? That is, after all, what you would do in a normal conversation.

The point about breathing is that normally you don't think about it. If you want to shout to someone at the end of the garden you automatically pull in more air to do it. If she is standing next to you you drop your voice accordingly. The moment you are told that you should be doing it in a certain way you become conscious of what you should be doing naturally. You have given yourself one more thing to worry about, when all you should be thinking about are the audience and the message.

Relaxation is another area where the pundits have a lot of advice to offer. One suggests that before going on stage you should tense your face muscles into a grimace and then relax them. 'Some people,' he adds helpfully, 'find it helps if they chew an imaginary toffee.'

Once again this is a distraction from the issues which you should be thinking about. You will be able to relax as much as you need to by being confident that you know your subject and have prepared yourself thoroughly.

Projection is a favourite word of the traditionalists. They talk about it just as drama coaches must have done to actors in the days before microphones. Obviously if you are going to be an opera singer, filling the Opera House in Covent Garden with your voice, you need to protect it from strain. To offer advice to business speakers, however, on 'pushing up air from their diaphragms' is patently inappropriate.

Similarly, it is ridiculous to try to get people to behave like actors by telling them to vary the pitch, tone and volume of their voices.

Actors learn these skills so that they can become other people and disguise their real personalities. This is exactly the opposite of the goal of the public speaker. You actually need to be yourself, talking as you do naturally. It also takes actors many years of training and even more of practice to become skilled at their craft – most public speakers do not have the time to devote to the construction of an act. Performing is not a career for them, even if the subject they are talking about is.

All the books on the subject of presentation effectiveness will give helpful suggestions on gestures you should make with your hands and ways you should stand – but how do you stand and gesture normally? If you are comfortable keeping your hands still, then that is what you should be doing, not waving them about because someone has told you it will help to get a message across or achieve emphasis. (Appearing on television might be one area where animated gestures need some control because of the restrictions of the screen).

It doesn't matter what you sound like

There is a general belief amongst traditional presentation advisers that speakers need 'elocution lessons', that they all need to be taught to speak in one particular style. We think this is not only wrong, but actually damaging to the individual who is being advised.

It doesn't matter whether speakers have accents which are unusual or even speech impediments, as long as you can understand them. And it doesn't matter whether they talk fast or slow, as long as they are speaking at the same rate as they would normally, and are not changing the way they talk simply because they are in front of an audience.

If the rate of idea presentation is correct, the chances are that when you come away from a conversation you will be able to remember most of what the speaker said. You will certainly be able to remember the key messages that were being put across. The fact that the speaker had an accent or speech problem will have helped to reinforce those messages by making them seem real and natural.

Casual conversation is not constructed in a literary way. People do not always finish their sentences. They repeat themselves. They use ungrammatical constructions – but they are obeying a different set of rules. They are obeying the rules of effective spoken communication which have evolved and been learnt, instinctively, down the ages.

From the moment you start to learn to talk you are testing different ways of catching people's attention and achieving what you want. If you want a drink, you learn how to ask your mother for one, and how to make sure she gets the flavour you want and brings it quickly.

All through your life you continue to build on those skills every day. Our coversational communication skills are likely to be far more practised in most of us than the literary skills which we learnt at school, and which we rigorously apply whenever we are asked formally to prepare any communication.

The power of eye contact and the need to get it right

Part of the success of normal spoken communication depends on eye contact. If you look at people as you make points they will listen and take notice.

If you look away too much you will appear shifty and unsure of what you are saying. If you look at them too much you will make them uneasy, appearing to be trying to stare them down.

In normal, informal conversation most people don't even have to think about this part of the communication. They do it naturally.

As soon as they get up on stage, however, they do something completely different. In some cases they will concentrate on their notes and completely ignore the audience. At other times they will stare wildly out at them. There is a way of getting the right, relaxed balance for the maximum impact.

Less eye contact, not more

The traditional wisdom contained in virtually all advice given about spoken communication is that the more eye contact the presenter can have with the audience the better. This dictum can be found in all the existing books.

We suggest that this isn't strictly true, because when people communicate informally the amount of time they actually look the listener in the eye is minimal. They look away from the listener whenever they are thinking about what they are going to say next, for example. While thinking we all tend to look up, down or to one side. We rarely look at our listener while we organize our next point.

The only time that it is essential to be looking someone in the eye is at the moment when the message concludes, so that you can see if you are getting a signal from the listener, such as a nod, which indicates that the message has registered.

This vital misconception has caused a lot of problems for many speakers, who force themselves to look at the audience as much as possible, especially at times when it would be far more natural to glance away.

If you can't communicate informally . . .

So for most people a careful study of how they communicate in informal conversation will show how they should be performing in a formal setting. In some cases, of course, people are bad communicators in all settings.

If this is the case they may need more fundamental assistance before they are able to consider giving formal presentations and speeches. That may involve considering if they're in the right job for their talents, or whether they need to find a way of increasing their self-confidence or assertiveness skills before trying to take on new responsibilities.

The Kingstree method has been particularly effective for successful and senior people who are already good communicators at a personal level.

The 'best man' syndrome

If the conversational form of communication is so successful, why does all the standard advice on public speaking require us to change everything when we stand up to make any sort of formal presentation?

Why is it that at a wedding the best man will be the most relaxed, witty and charming of people while sitting at the lunch table, but the moment he stands up to speak he buttons up his jacket, picks up his notes and begins to give a formal 'speech'?

The chances are that the people he was talking to earlier can remember everything he said to them, and were able to make a good assessment of the sort of person he was. Once he starts talking 'formally' the chances are that no-one will remember anything he has to say, and the communication will have been a failure.

Exactly the same thing happens throughout the business world, even at the most senior levels. Company chairmen, who in private are the most charismatic and persuasive of characters, become awkward, wooden and dull in front of an audience.

Everyone needs to find a way of maintaining his own relaxed, personal style of presentation, no matter what situation he finds himself in, because any deviation from that style is bound to be bad news. All the traditional views on how to make presentations result in deviations from normal behaviour and consequently detract from the speaker's performance.

What is an articulate person?

Even the traditional view of what constitutes an 'articulate' person is in our view suspect. If you ask people what they mean when they claim someone is articulate, they will tell you it is because that person puts together beautifully constructed sentences and paragraphs.

On the contrary, if you actually analyse the words of an articulate person, there will rarely be a complete sentence in sight. What there is, is clarity of thought and the use of concrete illustrations to make it easy for a listener to stay with the story.

Understanding this fundamental truth is the first step towards becoming a truly powerful and compelling speaker, and is one of the cornerstones of the Kingstree approach.

It doesn't matter what you look like – mostly

Many people misunderstand the sort of consultancy services which we offer. They think that we are involved in what is effectively 'cosmetics'. In other words, advising on how someone appears, how to dress and how to groom oneself. This is not our job.

Our job is to make absolutely sure that a client's key points and important messages come through loud and clear any time he or she is speaking to others, whether that is three people around a table or 300 in a big room, and that the personality comes through at the same time.

We try to avoid any comment to clients about how they dress or groom themselves, although once in a while we might notice a particular mannerism or style of dress that is distracting.

One client of ours was the head of a major British international company. Although he was always immaculately dressed and presented, he was known within his organization to have chest hair which frequently protruded over the collar of his shirt. We were specifically asked to deal with this problem.

It took me some time to figure out the right moment to raise the subject.

While preparing him for an annual general meeting, I was walking alongside this individual and I said, 'Say, what's that you've got there on your shirt collar?'

He immediately pulled his shirt collar up to cover the offending hair.

'Oh, I see,' I said, 'I thought the knot on your tie was frayed, but in fact what it is is some chest hair coming up over the collar. The solution is not to pull the collar up, the solution is scissors.'

That was the last time we saw that problem.

Once, in New York, I was invited to hear one of the most outspoken feminists of the day talking at a luncheon. I was astonished to find that out of the 400 people there, only about 15 per cent were women. In front of this almost entirely male audience, the guest speaker was dressed in a see-through blouse, with no bra underneath.

I can still remember how that woman was dressed, but I can't remember a single thing that she said. The speaker's dress sense had led her seriously astray by creating such a visual distraction!

Selling to The King of Wall Street

When *Business Week* put a picture of Salomon Brothers' chairman John Gutfreund on its cover, they christened him The King of Wall Street.

I had known him when I was in the banking business, and after moving to Europe I bumped into him at JFK airport, when we were both on our way to Paris, and told him what I was doing in London. He registered interest.

On my next visit to New York, I rang his office and asked for an appointment. I asked his secretary to tell him I was going to make him an offer he couldn't refuse. She rang back 20 minutes later to make an appointment for that afternoon, and a colleague and I went round to try to make a sale to this larger-than-life figure.

We were shown into one of Salomon's luxurious sitting rooms and John Gutfreund came in, puffing on his habitual cigar. 'So what's on you guys' minds?' he asked.

'Well, Mr Chairman,' I said, 'anyone talking to you in this room would have absolutely no doubt about what you said during that meeting, and absolutely no doubt as to what qualifies you to be chairman of Salomon Brothers.

'And yet we hear that as soon as there are a dozen or more people in a room you begin putting on an act and behaving differently, and that your personality no longer comes through.

'We're here because if you are prepared to spend 90 minutes with us once a month for six months, we could not only show you how to deliver a speech from a prepared text so that even your wife couldn't tell that you were reading it if she was sitting in the third row, but we could also give you some help on working from notes and headings and dealing with questions and media interviews.

'And on all those occasions you would come across in exactly the same compelling way that you do here in this informal setting, with your sense of humour, your willingness to laugh at yourself and so forth.'

John Gutfreund looked at us for a moment. 'Let me get this straight,' he said eventually, 'if I'm the worst speaker that you guys have ever dealt with, it is going to take me six of these 90 minute sessions to get cured. Is that right?'

'Yes,' I said, 'that's about right.'

'Okay. So that's nine hours.' He paused. 'If you can deliver on any one of those outrageous promises that you have just made, I will save that nine hours on the very first speech where I use any of your ideas. How quickly can you guys get started?'

His programme started the following week.

Using the approach in its totality

It is critical that anyone wanting to use our approach to communication should go through all the various stages, and does not simply pick up one or two of the techniques and use them out of context.

The training end of what we do involves a combination of intellectual and physical skills, and they have to be built gradually over a period of time, so that they can become second nature.

That is why, when we arrange for a client to have a number of sessions with us, we prefer to leave several weeks between each one, to allow time to assimilate what we have said and observe our principles at work in the way other people present.

The worst thing is for one of our clients to be thinking about our techniques while actually presenting in a high-stress situation. It is like addressing a golf ball on the third tee in an important tournament; you don't want to be thinking to yourself, 'Right, now I've got to keep my elbow in on the backswing' – it has to have become second nature before you get to that stage.

This was graphically illustrated when we were working with an exceptionally able 39-year-old executive, who had just been made head of one of the world's largest airlines.

We explained the need for a full understanding of the approach to him. But after the first 90 minute session, where our objective is simply to agree some basic principles, show the individuals how they talk in relaxed, informal conversation, and put in place a couple of initial building blocks to help with formal presentations in the coming months, he thought he could put what we had talked about into practice.

This young airline chief executive decided that he was now able to utilize our 'system' in a major presentation he was making a few days after the first session, addressing a very important audience.

He decided to ignore our warning that no-one should attempt to use the methods before becoming entirely familiar with them.

As a result his 20-minute speech ran for 45 minutes, and at the end of it several people came up to him and asked if he was feeling all right.

Needless to say, he blamed us entirely and was on the verge of firing us when we arrived a few weeks later to do the second session.

I reminded him that we had specifically warned him against doing what he had just done, and suggested that he should wait until the end of the second session before deciding whether or not to dispense with our services.

I'm pleased to say that the airline became a regular client, putting all its senior executives into our hands.

KEY POINTS

- Analyse the difference between your casual conversational style and your current presentation style
- Do not be talked into 'putting on an act'
- Do not give yourself extra anxieties about breathing and gesturing – do as you always do
- Watch how other people communicate in informal situations and how radically they change when 'presenting'
- Practise the right levels of eye contact – especially at the end of making a point
- Ensure clarity of thought before attempting a communication
- Ignore the grammatical rules of written communication
- Being 'natural' is a skill which can be learned
- Remove visual distractions
- Using the approach will pay immediate dividends. But do not use any of the techniques in isolation, without understanding the whole approach

· 3 ·

Effectively Projecting Your Personality

One of the keys to the Kingstree approach is teaching people how to project their true personalities through the way they speak.

As we said earlier, everyone does it naturally in relaxed, natural conversation. The difficult part is accepting that the same is possible in any situation, whether it is a one-to-one interview for an important job, or a speech to an audience of several thousand.

Personal chemistry wins business

In the end it is personal chemistry that makes people want to do business with other people. Very few of us, given a choice, will choose to work with someone we don't like or trust. If you are already successful to any degree the chances are that you already have a 'winning personality'.

In essence nothing should change about the way you come across when you stand up to speak. If you are different under those circumstances you may well be coming across as phoney, or boring and lacking in personality. As a result people will probably not like you and they certainly won't be convinced by, or remember, much of what you have to say.

Smiling isn't always the answer

Smiling is of course one of the keys to getting people to like you. If you are someone who never smiles, even in casual conversation, it is inevitable that you will be the same sort of person when presenting, and your personality will either work for you or not depending on how good you are at putting the case.

There is no point taking someone like that who is naturally dour, and training him or her to 'smile', because that would mean you were immediately going against the basic principle of the Kingstree approach, which is to make people be natural.

Apart from which it won't work, because the moment the adrenalin starts to flow, the speaker will forget everything we might have advised, will freeze and revert to his or her normal, solemn style. Someone who is like this all the time probably needs more in-depth help in the way of management development courses and tuition; the presentation problems are symptoms of something deeper.

In most cases, however, people are naturally very relaxed and pleasant in casual conversation, using plenty of smiles without even thinking about it. But as soon as they are put up in front of an audience they freeze, and they come across as stern personalities.

The too-perfect company chairman

One major British company has a chairman who, in most respects, fits perfectly the traditional image of an aristocratic business leader, but was giving totally the wrong impression of what he was really like.

We happened to see him interviewed on a major business programme on television, and we could see that he was being considerably less effective than he should have been.

This was because he became overly cautious about the way in which he expressed himself, working too intently to express each of his thoughts as perfectly packaged, grammatical sentences or paragraphs.

As a result he came across as patronizing and diffident, and seemed to be talking down or lecturing to the interviewer and listeners, when in fact he is the most personable, approachable and effective communicator imaginable.

By coincidence I had taped the interview because one of our other clients was appearing on it, so I rang the chairman in question and told him that I had seen the programme and that I thought there were a number of areas in which we could help him to improve his performance.

He immediately made an appointment, because he had already been criticized for this interview by his very supportive wife. We looked at the tape together and talked about the problems. By coincidence there was a film crew in the building who were going to tape a statement by the chairman for an internal video that they were making that morning.

After an hour of general discussion about talking to the media, I was then able to sit in on the taping of this internal video, and the chairman put into practice every bit of advice which I had just given him. As a result of using the Kingstree approach the whole segment could be filmed in one take, thereby saving everybody a great deal of time and money.

Building self-confidence

Everyone can, if he or she follows the system, smile and be natural even under pressure. The greatest contributing factor to this part of our approach is self-confidence.

For many presenters the confidence comes from knowing that they are doing well, that they know their subject, that their points are getting across and that the audience is listening.

Once the speaker has achieved those initial stages of the approach, the confidence begins to flood in and the speaker relaxes, smiles and allows his or her personality a freer rein.

Starting with the 'system'

The initial effect of the 'drill' which we start by teaching people to follow when they are delivering pre-prepared speeches, is that they begin to sound rather solemn.

It is hard to smile and be 'natural' when you are concentrating on learning and practising any mechanical skill or discipline.

It is like starting to drive a car; while you have to think about depressing the clutch every time you change gear, it is hard to talk naturally to someone in the passenger seat at the same time. Before long, however, with a little practice, you don't even have to think what your foot is doing, and you can concentrate on doing a number of different things at the same time – even talking on the telephone.

With the Kingstree system we teach clients how the pedals and gears function, and we stay with them until it becomes second nature. That is what gives them the confidence to overcome the nervous tensions which cause so many of the problems in spoken communication.

Sample speech

The following speech is an example which we like to use to illustrate how conversational you can be, even with a formal text. The speaker makes specific points, but they are illustrated with homely anecdotes to bring them alive and to invoke strong images in the minds of the readers. It is not enormously witty or clever, but it represents clear, simple communication in direct conversational language. It was written by Jack Heinz, one of the best speech-writers my father or I have ever worked with.

> *Ordinarily, we're all very serious about business . . . but when you think about it, it doesn't really have to be that way. You can be serious without being sombre . . . and you can be humorous without being frivolous.*
>
> *As a matter of fact, a lively sense of humour is a very old tradition at Bethlehem Steel. It goes all the way back to the founding of the company . . . because our founder, Charlie Schwab, loved a good laugh. Schwab 'had a million of 'em' . . . it was a big part of his charm. And he was at his best when the joke was on him . . . even if it had to do with a very serious matter.*
>
> *For example, he used to tell about the time when the company was just getting started and was terribly strapped for cash. It was really a matter of life and death. Schwab was desperate . . . so desperate that he went hat in hand to Philadelphia to see the famous banker, E.T. Stotesbury.*
>
> *Stotesbury listened to Schwab's story, and he wasn't at all impressed. Finally he said, 'I'll let you have half a million.'*

Schwab said, 'Oh, that's nothing at all. I can get half a million in New York and they don't even know me there.'

And Stotesbury said, 'That's the reason you can get it.'

So . . . you can see I'm right in step with company policy in bringing a light-hearted approach to some of the principles of successful business management.

Consider for example, the importance of good business ethics.

A young man, out of work and badly in need of a job, went to the proprietor of a country store. He claimed to be a hot salesman, and he was prepared to prove it.

The store owner said, 'All right, I'll give you a chance. There's just one flounder left in that barrel over there. If you can sell it, I'll give you a job.'

Well, a lady came in looking for a nice fish. The young fellow said he had just the thing for her and, with a big flourish, he reached into the barrel and brought out the flounder.

The lady looked it over and said it was rather large. Did he have anything smaller?

Indeed he did! He put the fish back, made a big show of groping around, and pulled it out again.

She said, 'Oh, that one looks too small . . . I'll tell you what . . . give me both of them!'

I think the moral of that story is perfectly clear . . . it just doesn't pay to try to fool a customer.

And I say this very seriously . . . every time someone in the business community pulls a fast one, he's handing ammunition to the critics of business . . . as well as the outright enemies of business.

So, all kidding aside, let's do business the way we want others to do business unto us!

One thing to remember in business, as in life itself, is that we can't always have things entirely our way.

Abraham Lincoln used to tell the story of the man walking down the street with two small boys who were crying their heads off. A neighbour heard the fuss and asked what was wrong.

The man said, 'The same thing that's wrong with the world . . . I have three of pieces candy and each of them wants two!'

That's life! There just aren't enough goodies to go around equally. The best we can do is find intelligent compromises, and try to be as fair and reasonable as possible.

KEY POINTS

- Your personality is your greatest asset
- Learn to project it, not to suppress it
- People do business with people – not with companies
- Only smile if and when it comes naturally
- The Kingstree approach will give you the self-confidence to become great
- Being conversational will allow the real you to come through

· 4 ·

How to Use Pauses and Silence

Many people make the mistake of believing that they 'talk too fast' when speaking in public. The actual rate of word delivery doesn't matter, (it is estimated that the average is 125 words per minute in English and 135 in French), as long as the words are intelligible.

The problem is that while the rate of word delivery is 125 per minute, the rate at which the brain operates is closer to 500 words per minute.

This doesn't mean that the words are coming out of a speaker's mouth too fast, it means that they are coming out of the brain too fast for the mouth to transmit, and the result is a conflict between thought and speech. What this creates in computer terms is an 'interface problem'.

As the mouth is talking about one thing, the brain is creating two or three additional and collateral thoughts which, from a structural point of view, may or may not fit with what is being said at that moment.

If the collateral thoughts, which are coming in quicker than they can get out, are added to the presentation, the audience becomes lost.

Some of the extra thoughts may even be more interesting than whatever the speaker set out to talk about in the first place, so the balance and structure of the presentation is drowned in a sea of ambivalent signals or potentially conflicting messages.

The brighter the speaker is, the bigger the potential problem. A very bright individual might be thinking at 700 or 800 words a minute, but the talk-speed remains at the standard 125–135 words per minute.

We have one client who is the head of a major international merchant bank. He is one of the brightest people I have ever worked with and has an astonishing grasp of his complex subject.

It is well known both inside and outside his organization that his presentations frequently come across as garbled, and that they in no way reflect the incisive, crisp thinking of which he is capable.

Our solution was to convince him that he firstly needed to organize a set of notes before a presentation, but even more important, that he needed to follow those notes rigorously, and allow no extra thoughts to get in.

That act of discipline leaves his brain free to concentrate on emphasizing the key points of his message rather than the spontaneous development of the subject matter in an inappropriate setting.

What matters are the pauses between the words

If your natural style is to spit words out fast, and people have no trouble understanding you in normal conversation, that is fine. But you must segregate a message into separate, discrete thoughts, then punctuate those thoughts with silence if you want people to understand in any depth, and remember what you have said.

No-one can speed-listen

Although people can teach themselves to speed-read, they cannot teach themselves to speed-listen.

For any listener, however educated he may be, or however keen he is to learn, there has to be time for the words to be processed by the brain, and digested after they have entered via the ear.

Allow time for mental digestion

If you don't allow time for that sorting and digesting process, the words which have already gone in will simply be pushed aside by the next ones, before the listener's brain has had time to sort them out. If the same pace is maintained to the end, then little or nothing will have stuck.

Effective presenters know how to transform the ear's inherent limits into a powerful advantage through using silence. Silence must always punctuate oral communication, to allow time for thought by the listener.

Silence is both a luxury and a necessity in spoken conversation, exactly as it is in music or poetry.

Pause before and after each thought

Pauses are necessary before and after each new thought to give the listeners time to digest what is being said, make a mental picture of it, and work out how any idea relates to them.

Pauses between thoughts also give a natural pace and proper emphasis to any speaker's message. The vast majority of presenters, however, doom their message to extinction by failing to pause long enough or often enough. Listeners cannot assimilate thoughts that are relentlessly run together. Each thought must be set apart.

Spoken communication has to be two-way, and the aim is to trigger a response in the mind of the listener with every major idea that is put across.

Allow time for the mental loop

If you say something which triggers a thought in the mind of the listener, it is no good if you then go straight on to the next point, without allowing the listener time to go out on a mental loop, processing and developing an internal image of whatever has been said.

Listeners have to be given time to do this and then come back to the speaker, having understood what has been said so far, and prepared to listen to the next thought or idea. By pausing you give them that time.

If you don't allow time for them to travel round the mental loop you will lose control of what the listeners are thinking about, and you will fail to get your message across. On the other hand if you don't give them something to think about, then you will not be able to involve them in whatever it is that you are talking about. If you don't involve them they won't remember a thing you have told them.

The effects of adrenalin on timing

Good communication depends directly upon the ability of the presenter to employ silence with confidence. For various reasons, even experienced presenters have a problem with this.

Speaking formally makes people nervous, and anyone who is nervous has a distorted perception of time. When you are standing up in front of an audience, you may think that every pause sounds like an eternity.

In reality, your silences may have been so slight the audience didn't even notice them, or at least thought they were part of your natural delivery.

Those few seconds spent searching your brain for the right word, which seem to be nowhere to be found, can seem like an endless agony to you. But if you ask anyone from the audience about it afterwards, the chances are he or she will have had no idea you were struggling at all.

This difference in the perception of time we call the Perceived Time Gap.

Even when presenters know that they should pause, they still find it hard to do so because they panic, making the adrenalin flow even faster. The faster the adrenalin flows the wider the Perceived Time Gap becomes, and the more they believe that a silence of a few seconds is never going to end. And the silence can actually intimidate them, and force them to charge forward before the audience is ready.

When people are put under stress, as they always are when making an important presentation, no matter how experienced they might be, the adrenalin will rush through their bodies to their brains.

On the whole, adrenalin is very useful, producing a nervous energy which makes great feats of strength, endurance and quick wittedness possible. Great acting performances, sporting successes and other heroic acts are all achieved with the help of adrenalin, which speeds up all the reactions and heightens the abilities. In a primitive setting, the sight of a charging tiger would hopefully produce enough adrenalin to allow someone to outrun the beast or take some other form of life-saving action.

The problem with this nervous energy for a presenter, however, is that it creates an invisible cocoon of distorted time. The cocoon wraps the presenter in a false impression that time is racing past. In reality nothing has changed except the presenter's notion of how fast the clock is ticking. In the grip of this illusion presenters invariably fail to deliver their message as a series of separate, distinct thoughts.

This notion of 'time passing quickly' often tempts speakers to speed up the rate at which they are delivering their thoughts, when they should in fact be doing the exact opposite.

The presenters, as a consequence, soon get out of step with their listeners, the human ears in the audience being simply unable to keep up with the rush of ideas.

It's rather like water poured too fast into a funnel. It all bubbles over the top and fails to flow through to storage.

KEY POINTS

- Segregate your message into discrete thoughts and then punctuate them with silence
- Allow the audience time for mental digestion
- Pause before and after each point
- Allow time for the mental loop
- Be aware of the perceived time gap
- Be aware of the brain-mouth interface problem

· 5 ·

How to Learn to Pause

When we are starting to train people in our approach we give them a written speech which they have never seen before, and we ask them to stand up and 'present it' to the audience.

The audience in this situation might be a few other people on the same course, or it might just be the consultant and a video camera in the case of our one-to-one training sessions.

Invariably the presenter will just read the piece straight through and, if experienced as a speaker, will look up every now and then to make eye contact with the audience in order to stress a point.

Because most of our clients are highly experienced speakers, they will probably be quite pleased with themselves when they reach the end, believing that they have done a good job with a difficult task.

Asked what percentage of the time they think they were actually making eye contact with the audience, they might say 30 per cent, or even 50 per cent. The chances are that the actual eye contact time was more like ten per cent, and was nowhere near enough. They should, in fact have been looking up from their notes for 80 or 90 per cent of the time, and glancing away for only ten or 20 per cent.

'Impossible', they say, 'how could I be looking at the script for only ten per cent of the time and still be reading it?'

But it is possible, in fact it is more than that, it is critical. The only reasons that they are unable to do it are that they are not pausing for long enough, and they are trying to pick up too many words at a time from the script.

A good presentation not a good 'reading'

Because of the way they approached the task at the first try, they did not give a good presentation. Although they probably gave a good 'reading' of the script, they will not have put across any of the messages which the writer intended, and they certainly won't have been able to imprint anything they said on the memories of the listeners.

Having filmed what they do in their own style, we then make them do it again, but this time they have to do a number of things for us:

1. AT NO STAGE MUST THEY SPEAK WHILE LOOKING DOWN AT THE PAGE.
2. THEY MUST ALWAYS PAUSE, FOR AS LONG AS THEY POSSIBLY CAN, BEFORE LOOKING DOWN AT THE PAGE.
3. THEY MUST ALWAYS PAUSE, AGAIN FOR AS LONG AS THEY POSSIBLY CAN, AFTER LOOKING UP FROM THE PAGE AND BEFORE SPEAKING THE WORDS.

So what they have to do is glance down at the page, take in as many words as they can (we call this taking a 'bite' of the text).

A bite can consist of just one word if that is all they are able to memorize, but it should rarely be more than five or six words.

If they try to pick up too many words in one bite it may be more than they can retain and that will cause them to panic.

Within reason they can take as long as they need to pick up these words.

A bite doesn't have to make sense on its own

This is purely a drill and we ask them to trust us, because however strange it seems at first to break sentences at points which are nongrammatical, it is a system which works for everyone, and they will soon be able to see why.

The pause for thought

Having picked up the words he is going to say, he must then make eye contact with the audience again, and pause briefly, before speaking the words which he has just read.

The point of that second pause is that it demonstrates that the speaker is thinking about whatever he is about to say.

That is flattering for the audience, and it also has them on the edge of their seats, as they wait to hear what is coming next and they will understand the silences to signal confidence on the part of the speaker. The audience's perception is that they are seeing someone who is thinking very carefully about what he is about to say, and the anticipation will be heightened even further.

If the speaker is worried about losing his place in the text, we suggest that he follows the words with a finger: the audience will not notice.

The 'did you get it' pause

The presenter then speaks the words that were picked up in the bite, and pauses – again for as long as possible.

This pause is saying 'did you get that?', and is allowing the audience time to take the words, build a visual image if that is appropriate, and compare the idea to their own experiences or feelings.

They cannot do any of these things if the presenter continues talking, because they will have to start listening again, and they cannot listen and think effectively at the same time.

After giving them a pause for thought with eye contact, (for as long as possible), the presenter can then glance down again, pick up another bite of words, come up, pause and do it again.

So the routine is always:

SPEAK THE WORDS
PAUSE WITH EYE CONTACT

LOOK DOWN AND TAKE IN THE NEXT WORDS
LOOK UP AND PAUSE WITH EYE CONTACT
SPEAK THE WORDS

And so on in a continuous loop.

To begin with this is very hard for most people to do. Firstly because they forget the pauses, secondly because if they remember the pauses they feel foolish, and thirdly because they become excited with their subject and want to rush on.

It takes practice, and constant nagging from the trainer to start with, to make sure that the pauses are always there.

Inside the speakers' heads it sounds ridiculous to have long silences punctuated with the odd word or phrase, and because of the effect of the adrenalin-induced 'time gap' the silences do sound very long indeed.

To the audience it doesn't sound anything like as strange. In fact it will hold them riveted as they wait for the next word or phrase to arrive.

Witnessing the difference

At the end of the second reading, the trainer will play back both readings on the television, and the trainee will inevitably be amazed by how different the second reading sounded. It will be more punchy, more authoritative, more memorable, and will make far more sense than he or she imagined when delivering it.

Because at this stage the drill is so rigid, there are bound to be some places where the sense of what is being said goes completely wrong, because of where the trainee started and ended the phrases picked up mechanically.

As the trainees become more fluent, we suggest that when a phrase is picked up which obviously doesn't make any sense without the words which came before, they can just repeat the last word or two from the previous bite. That will give emphasis and make the thoughts flow more naturally.

Ultimately, of course, it is going to be unrealistic to expect a presenter to talk in such a stilted and unnatural style. But as the trainees become more experienced, and begin to make the pauses naturally, their confidence will increase and they will be able to pick up more coherent chunks of the speech with each bite.

Even at its most unsophisticated this system still makes them better speakers than they were before. Later we introduce further refinements to allow the presenter to string together more words and smooth out the delivery.

Making pauses second nature

It is vital, however, that this basic technique becomes second nature, because it will form the foundation upon which everything else is built.

It will force the trainee to slow down and to allow the audience time to think. And it will ensure that everything which is said has a better chance of being remembered.

On top of those advantages, the technique has also given the audience the impression that the speaker is working from notes, not reading a script verbatim.

KEY POINTS

- Remember the 'pause for thought'
- Create anticipation in the audience
- Remember the 'did you get it' pause
- Pick up information from the page in bites
- A good 'reading' is a bad presentation

· 6 ·

Eye Contact

Pauses and eye contact reinforce the striking and staying power of every thought articulated by the presenter.

In normal conversation, people start and end significant points by looking at one another.

This invests what is being said with the appropriate value. It also means that the listener has to give some indication of whether the thought has been received and understood, and possibly, though not necessarily, whether it has been agreed with or not.

Once that reaction has been established, the speaker can then go on to draw conclusions or make another point, or the listener can become the speaker.

Eye contact demonstrates confidence in the message

If a speaker glances away while stressing or finishing a point, listeners tend to discount or dismiss the value of that particular thought.

For this reason, presenters in a formal setting must also make eye contact when a thought is started or ended. They must not be looking down at their notes, their feet or anything else which might suggest they are either not confident of what they are saying, or not telling the truth.

It is like the 'politicians' handshake', which is intended to demonstrate to you how pleased they are to meet you, and how much they want to make contact with you. If, while they are doing that, they are looking round the room to see who else is there, or if the moment they release your hand they move on to the next person, you no longer believe the message which the handshake was supposed to convey.

An audience's attention will always be dramatically influenced by a speaker's ability to pause and make eye contact at the conclusion of a thought.

At the same time it is possible to have too much eye contact. If a speaker in a casual conversation stares straight into the listener's eyes all the time that he or she is speaking, the listener is going to feel very threatened, uncomfortable and nervous, and will have to look away from the speaker, possibly missing what is being said as a result.

The same is true when speaking formally, and a way has to be found of getting the right balance of eye contact without staring the audience down and appearing unnatural. One of the main problems with most modern autocue or tele-prompt devices is that they lead speakers to look out towards the audience throughout the entire duration of the talk. Since the presenter is reading words directly from the clear screens to his left and right his own focus is roughly one metre in front of him, and he can rarely make true contact with the people in his audience, or accurately gauge their reaction.

KEY POINTS

- Start and end significant points with eye contact
- Watch the audience for signals of comprehension or non-comprehension
- Pauses plus eye contact equal drama

· 7 ·

Mixing Eyescan With 'Bites'

As the speakers become more experienced and confident with the basic technique, they can begin to streamline it, to vary the pace and create more continuity.

They can, for instance, start to mix a technique called 'scanning', with the orginal technique of taking 'bites' of the text one at a time.

To do that they must follow a different pattern:

THEY START BY TALKING AND LOOKING AT THE AUDIENCE

AS THEY SPEAK THEY BEGIN TO LOOK DOWN AND READ A FEW WORDS FROM THE TEXT

THEY LOOK BACK UP AT THE AUDIENCE TO DELIVER THE LAST FEW WORDS OF THEIR SENTENCE OR IDEA WITH DIRECT EYE CONTACT AGAIN

THEY PAUSE FOR AS LONG AS POSSIBLE WITH EYE CONTACT, INVITING THE AUDIENCE TO DIGEST THE IDEA, THEN . . .

THEY LOOK DOWN FOR ANOTHER BITE OF WORDS

THEY LOOK BACK UP AND PAUSE WITH EYE CONTACT
THEY SPEAK AND REPEAT THE EXERCISE

When the audience sees a speaker doing it this way, they assume that when the speaker's eyes go down for 'bites' he is looking at bullet points in his notes.

When he is eye-scanning and talking, the audience thinks he is just scanning his notes to stay on track.

The result is the same in both cases: they believe the speaker is working from notes, not simply reading a set script.

The speakers are now able to take larger bites of information, and consequently to make the words flow in a more natural way. They are also freer to inject their own personality into their words, having a less rigid and restricting formula to follow.

KEY POINTS

- Keep pausing
- Keep making eye contact
- Eyescans improve the flow and allow the personality of the speaker to come through

· 8 ·

How to Use Notes Effectively

Notes are by far athe best way to give most presentations, especially the less formal ones which virtually all executives give almost daily.

Some people think that it looks more impressive to be able to stand up and talk without any papers, believing that seeing people refer to notes will make the audience doubt that they truly know their subject.

This is quite untrue, and in reality there are very few people who are able to speak effectively without notes, except in the most informal of situations.

On the whole, audiences appreciate it if a speaker has made some notes, because it shows that he or she has put some thought into the presentation, has some specific points to put across, and is doing the audience the courtesy of not wasting their time by deviating from the central theme or key points.

Notes also give speakers the freedom of being able to wander around holding them, since there is no subterfuge involved. They are not confined to a lectern as is the case with a prepared speech.

We have already talked about the importance of eye contact, and it is just as important to be able to break that contact as it is to be able to hold it.

Without notes to look at, speakers who want to avoid staring at their audiences too aggressively will have to avert their eyes to something else. What are they going to look at? They might look at their hands or their feet, or they might stare out into the distance.

None of these alternatives are as satisfactory as being able to refer back to a set of notes whenever they want to look away from the eyes of their listeners.

A 'get ready' signal for listeners

Once the speaker has held a pause after a key point, the act of looking down at notes is actually very helpful to the listeners, because it provides punctuation. The look down says: 'here comes a new thought, get ready for it'.

Staying on track

The greatest benefit of all, however, is the ability of notes to keep speakers on track. Speakers all have moments when they lose their thread or are led off at a tangent. They might even forget whether they have covered a particular point, and go back over it by mistake.

It is all too easy for speakers to miss out vital parts of the message simply because they forgot them on the spur of the moment and didn't take time to check the notes.

Sticking to a predetermined running order changes all that. By noting down the points you want to cover, in the order you want to cover them, you provide yourself with a structure and a framework which gives a presentation shape and strength.

The Kingstree method with notes

Once trainees have mastered the Kingstree approach to set texts, we then ask them to prepare notes, so that they can speak on a subject for three to five minutes.

When they have prepared the notes, we ask them to go up to the lectern in front of the camera, and we film them as they introduce what they are going to talk about in their normal conversational style. They then deliver the speech from notes.

The reason why we film the conversational introduction is that at the end we want to be able to play them three different sections of film.

We already have film of them working briefly from a set text, delivering the message in a convincing and concise way, and we now have tape of them talking naturally, and another of them talking from notes.

With these three segments we can demonstrate to our clients that there does not need to be any change in communication style between the three. Whatever the situation they are in, scripted, using notes or talking spontaneously, they can still adopt their natural conversational style, and feel confident that it will work.

The common link between the three situations is the person's normal, relaxed conversational style, because that is the guiding light to what the presenter is really like, and that is what we want our clients to be like all the time.

By giving people a system for using notes we are providing them with one more weapon for their presentation armoury, and it is probably the most powerful one of all.

The pilot's checklist

The notes themselves should work in the same way as a pilot's checklist.

Many trained pilots are capable of flying their aircraft without the use of checklists, but they will always have them available and refer to them systematically because to miss out one vital action in the standard sequence of events could lead to a fatal disaster. I have myself experienced a serious problem along these lines when flying our company plane out of New York's La Guardia airport. So I use the checklist analogy with all our clients.

Trust your 'back brain'

Some people are nervous of using notes, and prefer to have their whole speech written out in full. They fear that their minds will 'go blank' when they look down and just see a few words which are meant to act as a reminder or trigger.

In reality this rarely happens. Provided the speaker is familiar with the subject matter, and has all the information stored in what we might call the 'back brain', that back brain will not let him down.

When the information is needed by the 'front brain' it might take a few seconds for the thoughts to sort themselves out and come forward. An untrained speaker might find those few seconds of silence too panic-inducing to be endured, but in fact they will provide a valuable opportunity to pause, during which the audience will actually be able to see the presenter thinking over and considering carefully what is going to be said next. Once again, it fuels their anticipation, and means that when the thoughts do come out, they will be given more weight or value.

Always trust your back brain not to let you down.

Don't be sidetracked

Enthusiasts, or people talking on subjects they know inside out, sometimes get sidetracked. Before long they are gushing out great streams of information which may be very interesting to them, but is not helping the audience to identify and retain the key messages.

Once again they have forgotten what the needs of the audience are.

If you have decided in advance, in the cool and calm of your office, what the best points are to illustrate your argument, and what order they should come in, then stick to those decisions.

The chances of being able to improve on those ideas on the spur of the moment, and with the adrenalin pumping, are very slight indeed. In fact you can be sure that you won't improve anything and you will frequently make it worse.

Stay with your notes at all times.

Think before you speak

Another problem is something we identify as 'talking while thinking'.

Always think through what you are going to say before you say it, otherwise you can end up saying some very foolish things.

The audience will be quite happy to wait a few seconds while you compose your thoughts, in fact they will be flattered that you are going to so much trouble on their behalf.

There is a terrible temptation for an inexperienced speaker to want to fill in any silences with words. Silence seems to intimidate, when in fact the silence would be much more effective and impressive.

The audience can't think about one point while you are continuing to talk unless they stop listening to what you are saying, which you don't want to happen. Similarly you won't be able to think clearly about the next point that you want to make if you are still talking about the last one. Take one thought or message at a time.

Talking while you compose the next idea invariably leads to waffle. Waffle should always be avoided because it will inevitably lead you off at a tangent, and it is always hard to get back on track. Furthermore, continuing to talk after you have completed one idea gives the audience an ambivalent signal. First they are not certain whether you have completed the previous idea or not, and they have to extract the next point out of many more words. Hence the message is substantially less concise, as well as being more difficult to follow.

Only one rehearsal

When you are using notes it is unwise to do more than one rehearsal, otherwise you will start to memorize the points and lose the spontaneity. That can lead to a feeling of panic when your memory seems to be failing you. Even if you can remember the next bullet point without looking down, you must still look down and check it, because the audience needs the punctuation for the reasons we have discussed, and you need it to stay on track.

Remember the previous lessons

The danger is that once you have made the notes and your brain is starting to run over all the familiar territories that you are going to be talking about, all the previous training on pausing and making it a two-way communication with the listeners flies out of the window.

Clearly, notes act as road signs of where you are going. But, used correctly, they also provide discipline.

The point of the notes is to keep you on track and to make you pause and look down every so often to see what should come next.

When you have seen what is coming next you should look up again, pause again for thought as you remember what the bullet point was put there to remind you of, and then talk about that point. For your listeners, a pause for thought will always add value to what you are saying.

KEY POINTS

- Notes provide freedom of movement
- They provide a 'get ready' signal for listeners
- They provide a logical focus for breaking eye contact
- They help to keep you on the pre-determined track
- They provide a structure and framework for the presentation
- Remember the pilot's checklist
- Trust your back brain
- Don't be sidetracked or allow yourself to digress
- Think before you speak
- Only one rehearsal whenever possible
- Keep the pauses and silences going

· 9 ·

How to Write the Notes

The way to write notes effectively is to start with the key messages which you are aiming to get across. There should not be too many of them, certainly not more than five, and preferably only about three in a 15–20 minute presentation.

These are the points which you have decided you want the audience to remember. Limit the number, or you will not get your message across. This can be quite painful for some people, because they may have 20 or even 50 points which they feel compelled to include. But they must cut back ruthlessly, otherwise all their efforts will be wasted.

When you are prime minister

I was with the chairman of a major oil company one day, trying to explain why it was important to limit the number of key messages in any one communication.

He was an excellent speaker in a traditional way, but we just couldn't cure him of putting too many points into his speeches.

I remembered a story I had been told about Lloyd George when he was Britain's Prime Minister, and thought it was would illustrate the point nicely for him.

Harold Macmillan, who was then a newly elected member of parliament, went up to Lloyd George in the House of Commons one day and asked how many points he should have in his maiden speech. Lloyd George replied; 'Well, you have only just arrived, so I would strongly recommend that you limit yourself to one key point, so that when the old men like me are talking about the speech afterwards, we can encapsulate in one phrase what your speech was about.

'When you have been re-elected a few times it might be possible to add a second point to your speeches and I, as Prime Minister, can occasionally allow myself the luxury of a third point.'

My client looked at me for a few moments and then grinned and said: 'But I am the chairman.'

Too many ideas

I once attended a lecture by one of America's most eminent academics. It was the most brilliant dissertation on the state of the planet and the future of us all, filled to the brim with ideas, facts, predictions and statistics.

I was very impressed until a few hours later, when I tried to remember some of the points which he had made. I could remember nothing specific.

He had given me no time to absorb one idea before hitting me with another, and he had given me no visual mechanisms for locking the pictures in my memory. He had established no theme or framework and the isolated thoughts were delivered with complete lack of regard for the audience's ability to take in the message.

So the first discipline is to cut the messages down to the minimum, on the assumption that if the audience wants to know more they will raise the subjects during the question and answer sessions.

If they don't raise questions relating to what you have said, it's a pretty good bet that you lost their attention along the way, either by including too many points or by running one idea into another and making your listeners have to work to keep up.

Written material for back-up

If it is a very complex subject that you are going to talk about, then you should prepare written material which you can hand out at the end. Anyone wanting to know more can then delve into the meat of the subject, having been tempted by the key messages of your presentation.

Use bullet-points

Put your three key points down in the right order, and then make a bullet-point note for every single point you are going to make, or examples you aim to include in support of those key messages.

A bullet-point should be as close to one or two words as you can get, while still allowing you to recognize what it is there to remind you of.

If you put down a full sentence you end up reading it out verbatim, which will defeat the whole purpose of the notes.

If you put down part of a sentence it may not make sense to you when you come to glance down at your notes, with the adrenalin pumping through your system, and you may then panic.

If, however, you choose the right trigger word or words, your brain won't let you down, it will bring the right information to the front when you need it, provided you trust it to do so. It may be three or four words if that is as small as the trigger will go, but the key test is whether you can pick up what it is about from one quick glance.

Use a lot of bullets

There is also a danger with speakers who are too confident of their material, that they will not give themselves detailed enough notes.

While each note should always be as brief as possible, there should also be a lot of them, particularly in the areas of the subject where you are most knowledgeable because that is where you are in the most danger of going off on personal hobby horses, and recounting anecdotes which are coming back to you as you talk.

The chances are that you will be feeling totally at ease during all this, but the audience is beginning to wonder what you are talking about.

If you do have a last-minute thought as you enter the room or walk up onto the stage, and you are sure it is important, take the time to make a note of it in the margin of your notes at the relevant place, but don't just launch into it out of context.

KEY POINTS

- Identify key messages
- Control your rate of ideas
- Prepare written material for back-up
- Use a lot of bullets

· 10 ·

The Listener is the Driving Force

It is not what you say in a presentation that is important, it is what the audience thinks about what you have said that matters.

You could have given them the most reasoned argument in the world, backed up by a wealth of detailed research material and statistics, but if the audience goes away in the belief that you don't know what you are talking about, or if they go away not understanding what you are talking about, you have given them totally the wrong message.

You might as well have stayed at home.

The pace and speed of good spoken communications are driven by the recipient of the message, not the transmitter.

Respect the needs of the listeners

If someone stands up with a speech that has been written in advance, and proceeds to read it out from beginning to end, that person is not taking into account any of the needs of the listeners.

All that speaker is doing is forcing a message and format onto the listener or audience, regardless of whether they want to hear it, whether they understand it, or whether they are paying attention.

You would never be able to get away with that in a casual conversation, unless you were the most insensitive of bores.

When you are talking to someone in a relaxed setting you adjust your message as you go along, depending on the reaction that you get from the listener.

Every so often he or she will make a sound or give a nod, which will not necessarily indicate agreement, but will indicate understanding of what you have said so far and readiness for the next part of your message, signalling you to move on.

By watching their faces and listening to the sounds they make, you are also able to tell if they are agreeing or disagreeing with you, whether they are fascinated or bored, whether they like you or dislike you, and you adjust the speed and content of your message to fit reactions as you go along.

You don't even have to think about this if you are a skilful communicator. It is second nature and happens automatically.

The best communication, therefore, is being driven by the listener and not, as is generally assumed, by the speaker.

While it is not possible to maintain the same degree of listener sensitivity once the audience consists of more than a few people, it is still crucial to plan and design the communication from the listener's point of view, not the speaker's.

By examining what is actually going on at the recipient's side of the communication, we can begin to draw some conclusions about what needs to happen on the transmission side, if the communication is to work.

These views are, in my opinion, absolute. Just as fixed as the laws of gravity. If the audience isn't listening, hearing and comprehending, then the communication will be a failure.

Helping listeners find what they want

If listeners are expecting to hear some valuable information, they will perceive it much more quickly when it is delivered than they will if they do not know what to expect.

If, in other words, you give clear signposts about what your message is and how it is going to be structured, that will leave the listeners free to focus on what you are saying that is in line with what they expect the message to be.

Looking for a needle in a haystack is hard enough, but if you don't even know what you are looking for it will become impossible. The principle is that looking 'for' something is much easier than looking 'at' something – and the same applies to listening.

It is impossible for people to remember everything that they hear, so they must endeavour to remember what is most important. A speaker can help them to do this by pointing out the most important things.

What are your goals?

In our view, good presentations achieve two goals: first, the audience retains some new information; second, the audience gains a true impression of the presenter's basic attributes and personality.

Achieving both goals is vital because listeners become convinced by making both objective and subjective judgements. Successful presentations allow listeners to consider what is being said and to develop a solid impression of the presenter.

Talking naturally

Being natural, therefore, is the key to communicating well, because listeners will respond much better to presenters who 'talk' their message, than they do to presenters who 'give a speech'.

A speech in the traditional sense is often an exercise in stilted behaviour, whereas a talk permits the audience to hear and see the presenter communicating as he or she would in a relaxed setting such as an office, home or restaurant.

The personal experiences and knowledge of each listener will also influence perception of the presenter's style and message. Anyone who forgets or neglects these realities will fail to achieve his or her objectives.

Listeners have in-built limits which the presenters must respect.

Knowing the limits

The limits that govern presentations derive from the way people obtain information. Roughly 95 per cent of the brain's total input of information comes in via the eyes. Smell, taste, touch and hearing together account for a mere five per cent of accumulated brain data.

The human ear is an inefficient device for gathering information, yet when a message is correctly communicated orally it is the most effective means of transmission.

Figure 1

As children we often want to have stories read to us by our parents, even though we might be able to read them faster ourselves. We like the human contact, and listening to someone else's voice changing emphasis and intonation can bring things alive in a way which might not happen on the printed page. (Clients and colleagues all tell me that employing the Kingstree approach to bed-time stories makes them even more enjoyable for their children!) No matter how skilful you are at writing a message, it is difficult to make people want to read or remember it.

If, on the other hand, you are speaking to people, you can make them want to listen, and if you do it skilfully enough you can compel listeners to process, understand and then remember what you are saying. That is because listening requires more effort than reading. Because it requires effort on behalf of the listeners they feel personally involved in the communication, and anything which they hear and understand, they will actually 'own'. It would be easier for them to dismiss something which they have read as being nothing to do with them.

So oral presentations offer an unrivalled opportunity to communicate effectively, and must be organized for delivery in a way which takes into account how the ear operates.

Remember that, as discussed in Chapter 4, people can talk much faster than audiences can listen. The consequence is that most presenters unwittingly overwhelm their audiences with an avalanche of thoughts.

Presentations should consist of a series of separate and distinct thoughts. Listeners must be given enough time to absorb each thought before the speaker moves on to the next one, so that they can relate it to what they already know or feel about the subject. If they are not given adequate time to evaluate each thought as it is spoken, they will steadily lose interest and finally stop listening.

The rhetorical question

The rhetorical question was invented with the intention of getting the audience involved in what is being said, by getting them to do something. They are encouraged by the question to think up their own answers, which makes them concentrate on the message and anticipate how the speaker will answer it.

While they are doing so the speaker pauses, allowing the listeners to think, and then comes back with the right answer – which hopefully matches theirs.

That is exactly how an effective speaker should operate – by involving the audience, with whatever combination of devices is needed.

If the speaker puts too many points into the communication, or runs them together, without segregating ideas to allow the audience time for reflection, or introduces a conflict between spoken and visual messages, the audience will stop listening because they will feel left out, or at best feel they are being 'talked at' rather than 'talked *with*'.

The ear is like a short, narrow funnel and can take in words and convey them properly to the brain only as long as its severe limitations are respected.

So anyone preparing to speak to others must be clear what it is that they themselves want to say. They must ensure that they keep the messages as simple as possible. They must make sure that everything they say is understandable to the audience, and that the audience has time to understand.

The stages so far

The first stage is the use of pauses and silences.

The second is to create an impression of thoughtfulness and spontaneity by not being seen to read a script, or by using notes.

The third is to give as much thought as possible to who your audience are, what their needs are and how those needs fit in with yours.

Sample speech

This speech is an introduction to another speaker. It is being delivered by a senior executive of a major bank to a group of new recruits. These recruits have been through the most rigorous of selection procedures in order to get into this organization, and the speaker has the job of catching their attention and making a potentially dreary introduction of a distinguished guest speaker exciting.

Some time ago, Lord Shawcross, Danny Davison, Morgan's London Manager, and I took the morning train to Cambridge. It was the Bank's first recruiting effort in the United Kingdom and we had scheduled five candidates. After two unproductive interviews a very attractive third year law student arrived. His opening comment was that he had utterly no interest in any aspect of banking.

His sole reason for appearing that rainy morning was to spend 45 minutes with Lord Shawcross.

During the next three quarters of an hour, Danny Davison and I listened to the young lawyer interview Lord Shawcross about his experience as Chief British Prosecutor at the Nuremburg trials; his later period as Attorney General under Clement Attlee, and his exploits as an active member of the international sailing fraternity.

Just as Davison and I were convinced that the young law student might have been won over at least to consider the prospects of a career at Morgan, he thanked us and left. We never saw him again.

I'm delighted to report that since our inauspicious start with the young Cambridge law student, we have hired 130 Morgan bankers from universities here in the United Kingdom. Today these 130 people serve all over the world and represent nearly ten per cent of all the Bank's professional staff.

Since that trip to Cambridge, Lord Shawcross has continued to distinguish himself by serving as a director of a number of major companies, including Shell, Hawker Siddeley, EMI and Times Newspapers. He is also a chancellor of Sussex University.

Lord Shawcross has been a key member of Morgan Bank's International Advisory Council for 18 years. That group comprises top business leaders from every important industrialized country.

It is with great pleasure that I introduce our speaker this evening, the distinguished Lord Shawcross.

KEY POINTS

- Be aware of the audience's needs
- Watch what they are telling you
- Know the limits of listening
- Use rhetorical questions
- Talk naturally
- Involve the audience
- Make the subject relevant to them

· 11 ·

Making Your Messages Memorable

Some of our clients come to us as a result of surveys which their companies have done into how much people actually remember after a series of management or staff meetings.

In the majority of cases the attendees remember very little of what was said, and often have trouble reproducing even the key points weeks, or perhaps days later.

There is clearly no point in talking to people formally or informally if they aren't going to remember what you are saying.

There is less point in spending a great deal of time and money preparing a major conference, and taking everyone away from their desks to attend, if they do not come away with any lasting messages.

What do they want and need to know?

Before you start to prepare a spoken communication with anyone, you should seriously consider what it is they need and want to know.

Once again it is easy to see a parallel in ordinary conversation. Imagine a man arriving late at a dinner party. After making his excuses he tells an amusing anecdote of how his car broke down on the way there. The story is full of insights into how one feels in such a situation, which are recognizable to everyone else at the table. As a result, everyone has a clear picture of what happened to this person to make him late; they are amused, they get a good impression of his character and they are completely ready to excuse the tardiness.

How different it would have been if the same latecomer had launched into a long dissertation on how he got stuck in traffic, with a detailed account of traffic statistics and the comparative advantages of different routes.

Everyone has met this type of person, and been on the receiving end of this sort of monologue. The result in most cases is boredom, because although the speaker is interested in the alternative routes which could have avoided the traffic jam, the listeners, who had no such problem that evening, are not interested.

The speaker is talking about a subject which interests him but does not interest the listeners. The chances of anyone remembering anything which he says are minimal, because the speaker has done nothing to get the listeners involved.

In a business setting it might be a computer expert asked to give a presentation on a new software product to a group of potential clients. The expert, being an enthusiast for the subject, launches into long descriptions of the technology involved, and just why it is the most brilliant in the world, when the audience actually wants to know whether it will get the invoices out quicker or improve customer care.

If the speaker addressed those questions with concrete illustrations of how the improvements would happen, the talk would probably be shorter and a lot more valuable to the recipient. By tackling it from the wrong angle the message is not understandable to the audience and is consequently not memorable. The chances of making a sale if the audience can't remember what you have said about the product are minimal.

The clever conversationalist gets the other person to speak first, in order to find out what his or her interests are, and then couches everything in terms designed to interest the listener.

If the speaker is interested in fishing, and has just come back from a wonderful week chasing big game fish off the Florida Keys, he or she needs to find out if the listener is more interested in fishing, boats or travel, before launching into stories about the trip. Otherwise there is a risk of making the listener tune out at the beginning of the conversation, and it is then almost impossible to retrieve the situation.

Do your background research

The same applies in a formal setting, except that in most cases you have the advantage of having time to plan what you are going to talk about in advance. You may not be able to talk to each of the listeners personally before the speech, in order to find out about their likes and dislikes, but you can research them as a body.

If you are talking to a conference, for instance, you need to know what has brought them to the conference hall in the first place. If you are addressing an internal company meeting, you need to know the hopes and concerns of the other people there, before you can hope to say anything which will have any impact on them.

Starting strong

My colleague Alistair Grant was holding a group course at which a structural engineer was explaining how strong you should make an aircraft. Within the first few seconds Alistair was unable to understand what he was talking about because he could not focus on what was being said.

On the second day, having had the problem explained to him, the engineer started the same talk again. This time he started it by asking the audience if they had ever held a Coke can in their hands. If they had, he continued, they would know that it was not very strong. What they might not know was that the thickness of the aircraft was only four times the thickness of the Coke can.

He then developed the theme by saying that if a car goes over a pot-hole in the road you expect it to survive. If it goes over a cliff you expect it to be a write-off. He went on to explain that the aircraft company applied the same principles to the design of its planes, expecting them to survive certain things but not others.

The point was that by starting in an anecdotal way, relating a complex subject to an every-day example which could be recognized by everyone in the audience, he was able to make what he was saying understandable and fascinating. If you can arouse the curiosity of the listeners in the first few moments, they are much more likely to listen to you.

Getting straight to the point

Analogy and illustration isn't the only way to make a strong start, of course, it is only one good way. There are others. Sometimes such an approach could actually cause a negative reaction within the audience.

Suppose, for instance, you are called in to brief the boss on something. The boss is in a hurry, and you start by telling an illustrative anecdote. The chances are you will be told to stop wasting time, and to get on with the facts.

In many other circumstances it is advisable to go straight into the main message, because that is what the audience is there for, and what they are waiting to hear. It is the classic formula of:

TELL THEM WHAT YOU ARE GOING TO TELL THEM
then
TELL IT TO THEM
then
TELL THEM WHAT YOU HAVE JUST TOLD THEM

Cut out the platitudes

One way not to start any talk, however, is with platitudes and soothing words – How nice it is to be here once again, It is a great honour to be here in your beautiful city, I'm particularly grateful to you, Mr Chairman, for extending me this invitation to speak – you may be putting the audience at their ease, but you won't be attracting their attention, and you might even encourage them to doze off!

Making it personal

If listeners can't relate what you are saying to something personal in their own lives, they will have trouble remembering it. If you are talking about the experience of going through a divorce or being involved in a car crash with someone who has had a similar experience, it is easy to make your thoughts and feelings on the subject pertinent and memorable.

If you are talking to someone who has no prior experience of your specific topic, you are going to have to think of other experiences which he or she might have had which would be similar, and draw parallels which will bring what you are saying alive.

Sample speech

The following sample demonstrates how to start strongly with vivid images which will mean something to everyone in the audience, but which will initially seem unconnected and therefore puzzling. Long pauses increase the drama and the intrigue. It is being delivered by a senior head of department at Salomon Brothers.

Fabergé Eggs.
Eastman Kodak.
Ming Vase.
Tabriz Carpet.
Matisse.
Gainsborough.
IBM.
Pan AM Building.
What do all these have in common? They all represent investments that have produced substantial returns to their holders.

Four years ago Bob Salomon took the innovative approach of comparing the rate of return of so-called 'collectables' with the traditional investments such as stocks and bonds.

Bob has always been an innovator in two additional ways . . .

He has pioneered analysis of the relationships between various types of markets, and the effect of those relationships on portfolio planning.

When Bob left US Trust to join the family firm in 1965, Salomon Brothers had been known as a real power in the debt markets since the turn of the century. We had also been recognized as very good Equity traders.

It is through Bob's hard work and innovation that we finally have an Equity Department that we can be proud of!

Making abstract ideas imaginable

Many of the concepts which managers have to talk about are hard for people to grasp the first time they hear about them. Take the idea of 'quality' for instance, which is something that virtually every company is trying to instil in its workforce at the moment.

As a concept, quality is pretty hard to picture, but people can visualize the car they once owned whose wing mirror fell off every time they slammed the door.

If the speaker starts by asking them to picture that car, and is able to describe the picture in an amusing fashion, without losing its serious element, then he has caught the audience's attention, and put a more understandable face on a concept which might otherwise have remained just a word to them, an abstraction.

Create mental pictures

Words do not stick in people's memories on their own, they must be attached to mental pictures or memories. The real issue in spoken communication is what the audience thinks about what is said.

By creating a concrete example to illustrate a concept, and by telling it in a dramatic and, hopefully, a witty way, a speaker can cement an idea in the minds of the listeners. It is then possible to move on to broaden an analogy or to make it more complex, provided the listeners are taken through each step at their own pace.

It is like painting pictures with words. The thing to remember, however, is that the same words will conjure up different pictures for different people.

If you ask an audience to picture the 'Wild West' for instance, one person might have a romantic vision of a camp-fire under the stars, and a bunch of 'real men' alone with nature and their horses. Another person might remember the slaughter of the Indian tribes, and the squalor and greed of the goldstrike towns with their bars, brothels and diseases; while another might think of the Lone Ranger. Whatever the mental pictures evoked by the mention of 'Wild West', they will be very vivid because they are part of each audience member's own library of memories and images, which make up part of a mental databank.

It is relatively easy, of course, to evoke emotive images of something like the Wild West, but the same theories are absolutely valid when you are talking about the most arcane, technical subjects.

When an expert on a given subject mentions a particular piece of equipment the listeners who have some knowledge on that subject automatically trigger in their own minds a stream of thought processes provoked by the image they have in their minds.

If the audience does not have in-depth knowledge of the subject, then the speaker needs to find a connection with something they do know about. If, for instance the talk is about the chips which go inside electrical goods, then the image might have to be of a stereo system or television or personal computer, anything of which the audience has direct experience and which provokes vivid images in their minds.

Given the right stimulus, an audience will create more powerful visual images for itself than the speaker can provide on a screen or in hand-outs.

Don't be afraid of clichés

Some people are very nervous about using clichés in spoken communication. In most cases they shouldn't worry. Your main concern should not be to dazzle people with your imaginative use of language; your main concern is to make yourself understood, and to make your words memorable. While clichés may be bad in written communication, they can help in avoiding misinterpretation in spoken communications.

Clichés have become clichés because people use them all the time. People therefore understand immediately what you mean when you use them.

If you talk about 'not seeing the wood for the trees' or 'the best thing since sliced bread', you can be sure that everyone in the audience understands the same thing by the words as you do. They may cringe at it, but at least they won't be wasting time trying to work out what you are talking about.

Always prepare

There is a misconception amongst very senior people, both in business and government circles, that if they are high enough up in their professions, and have enough experience behind them, they will be able to stand up and speak about their subject for fifteen minutes without doing any preparation.

People who are less confident of their own abilities to present are likely to go to a great deal of trouble to prepare themselves and, provided they go about it the right way, their hard work will bear fruit.

Those who are over-confident of their abilities, particularly people senior enough not to have anyone in their organization brave enough to tell them what a bad job they are doing, are more likely to start rambling off at tangents, failing to make succinct points crisply, and repeating themselves.

Lack of preparation will not only result in an ineffective presentation, it can actually insult the audience.

One of the benefits of our approach is that it cuts preparation time down to the bare minimum, because it provides some rules for structuring and for keeping messages simple, but we would never recommend that anyone should get up to speak without doing some serious thinking beforehand.

That does not mean that they have to write themselves a complete script – that will almost certainly be unnecessary in the case of people who really know their subject. But it does mean that they must ration themselves on the amount of information they are planning to impart, and be clear in their minds what their key messages are.

The more senior and experienced they are, the harder that is going to be. How do you distil a life-time's experience into three key points?

But that is virtually what has to be done if an audience is to be able to follow what is being said.

That means sitting down and thinking:

1. What message would be most useful to this audience?
2. What is the audience's level of understanding of the subject likely to be?
3. How can I best get the message across and illustrate the points I am making in a vivid way?

The chances are that in most cases this sort of structured thinking will result in a set of notes of the type we have already described. The speakers must then ensure that they stick to the notes and don't allow themselves to wander off down other avenues of their memories, experiences and ideas.

KEY POINTS

- Research what the listeners want and need to know
- Prepare messages thoroughly in your mind
- Start strong
- Go straight to the point
- Cut out the platitudes
- Make it personal to them
- Make abstract ideas imaginable
- Get them to paint mental pictures
- Never fear clichés

· 12 ·

Avoiding Digressions and Distractions

By working to notes it is possible to structure a presentation in advance, and know that you will not miss out anything important when the adrenalin starts pumping.

This is very helpful to the inexperienced and unconfident presenter.

The dangers of digressing and distracting the audience are greater, however, amongst people who are confident of their subject, comfortable with the situation and having a good time.

Confident presenters talking to interested, responsive listeners, run the risk of talking too long and trying to say too much.

Even the most intrigued audience will begin to lose its ability to remain attentive to the same presenter after about 20 minutes. Psychologists suggest that the attention span of a group of people listening to one speaker is actually only 18 minutes.

Limiting the number of points

Similarly, audiences shouldn't be expected to remember more than three or four major points in that time span.

If the material requires longer than 20 minutes to present, it would probably be wise to involve more people in delivering the material. This provides the listeners with more than one personality to engage.

Structuring presentations

There is no universal, unchanging way to structure a presentation. Formats vary according to several determining factors such as different objectives, audiences, surroundings and presenters.

But there must be an underlying structure of some sort.

The decision to use a prepared text or to talk from notes, and the desirability of using visual aids, should be determined by considering factors like the time constraints, the possible legal implications and, once again, the specific objective.

Since presentations are frequently intended to persuade by virtue of winning the listener's agreement, presenters should pinpoint how they want their listeners to react, and then work backward step by step, to formulate a tailored approach.

Prepared texts, for instance, are useful when presenters have to cope with a strict time requirement or when their material is sensitive.

The dangers of spontaneity

People who speak spontaneously run the risk of rambling and making half-considered comments. Notes can often neutralize this tendency because they serve as a firm guide, as well as a specific reminder of points to cover.

A full text can also be a great tool for anyone who has to repeat the same presentation a number of times, for instance a 'road-show', where financial or other information is delivered to a number of locations in a short space of time.

Most people believe intuitively that if they deliver the same message repeatedly they will eventually know it 'by heart', and will then require no use of notes or scripts. Our experience suggests that the reverse is true. Over-familiarity with the subject, leading to few references back to notes or script, is a prescription for disaster.

Failure to stay with the original script generally leads to inconsistent performances at best, and normally results in key points being either repeated, or worse, entirely left out.

Deviating from one's notes or script can also lead to material misstatements. We have seen any number of examples where an overconfident presenter failed to refer to the text and said billion instead of million, or inadvertently changed a negative into a positive.

The real problem here is that the presenter generally won't realize the error, while audience members who are paying attention will know immediately.

The Kingstree approach to ad-libbing

Having said that we rarely advise people to talk without any notes, there are obviously going to be some situations where even brief notes would be too formal and inappropriate.

If you are asked at short notice during a board meeting to describe what you are doing about a particular project, the chances are that you will have no notes and that you will know enough about the subject to be able to talk off the top of your head.

The audience will probably be leading you with questions in a situation like that anyway, so you will have to respond to their agenda, not follow any preconceived plan of your own.

Still prepare

As soon as there is any formality involved, however, it always pays to prepare, even if you want to seem to be ad-libbing.

Suppose, for instance, that you are at dinner and just as the meal is ending you are asked if you will stand up in a few minutes and talk.

The best approach, if you have time, is to make a few notes of the key points you want to make (say, on your place-card or even on the cuff of your shirt – hence the phrase 'off the cuff') which you can refer to once you are on your feet.

Even if you are confident about what you are going to say while sitting thinking about it, the arrival of the adrenalin in your system as you stand up may wipe everything out of your mind.

For your own self-confidence you need to have a few trigger words jotted down, to get you started and keep you on track.

Keep using the pauses

All the techniques incorporating the use of pauses and eye contact apply, however, even when you are ad-libbing. Even if you don't have notes to refer to, you will need to pause in order to compose your thoughts, to be seen by your audience to be thinking about what you are saying and to give them time to digest what you have said.

If you are not using notes at all you will e in a situation which genuinely resembles normal conversation. In the course of a conversation you break eye contact with the listeners in a number of ways, some of which convey strong, positive messages, some of which appear shifty, some of which convey no signal at all.

Sometimes, for instance, you might just look down at the floor as you compose your thoughts, or at your hands. At other times you will be looking up but your eyes will appear to be focused on your thoughts rather than on the listener. There is only a flicker of difference between focusing into someone else's eyes and just short of them, but the effect is dramatically different for the listener.

Strong, definite movements are better than a constant, nervous shifting of the focus, which can make someone look frightened, or possibly even dishonest. Too much deliberate sweeping from side to side of the audience can look false and contrived.

It is easier to move the eyes around naturally if you are walking around the platform, even if only a little, since your gaze will automatically move with you. The real trick is to have in mind the key, points, just as if they were written down, then work to maintain the discipline of limiting your remarks to the intended issue.

Never ad-lib for real

Real ad-libbing is to be discouraged, (for all but the most foolhardy). The chances are that anyone who feels confident enough to do it is, in fact, over-confident and riding for a fall. It might, for instance, be the chairman of a major company who has no-one around him with the nerve to point out how unstructured and rambling his speeches are.

One of the reasons that senior executives hire us at Kingstree is because they know we will not hesitate to tell them when and how they could improve their performances, and one of the quickest ways to do that is to make sure every ad-lib is carefully planned.

KEY POINTS

- Limit the number of points you are going to make
- Never add more on the spur of the moment
- Don't become over-confident
- Always prepare – even when ad-libbing
- Never ad-lib for real

· 13 ·

How to Prepare a Presentation

Once you are a confident practitioner of the Kingstree Approach, you will be able to prepare presentations in the minimum time; the amount of time, in fact, that it takes you to work out what your messages are and how you are going to articulate them.

Nor do you need to spend hours rehearsing. In fact, over-rehearsing could well impair your final performance. In addition, you probably need fewer and simpler visual aids than you have used in the past, since they too could detract from the impact of what you have to say.

The worst thing that could happen by going over a presentation too many times is that you will become bored with your own material. If you are bored, then you will communicate that feeling to the audience even before you start. You might also be tempted to change or modify one section simply because you have become bored with the examples you have included.

By relying on a text or notes and not being over-rehearsed, you will be able to sound spontaneous and conversational. It isn't hard to sound natural if you are allowing the words to come into your mind for the first time and, provided you are fully familiar with the ideas and the messages which you want to put across, they always will come. But, it takes a considerable acting talent to take a memorized speech and make it sound as if you are saying the words for the first time. Few, if any, of our clients can do that.

Furthermore, being over-rehearsed often leads to over-confidence, or a sense that it's not necessary to consult one's notes. The worst part of the over-training or over-rehearsal process is that it leads people to change examples, or to deviate from a track which was originally chosen. Any of these eventualities can result in disaster.

Whether you are writing the speech out in full, or making notes to talk from, there are some basic rules of preparation to follow.

Start strong

Always begin strongly. Your opening is your point of maximum impact because everyone will be willing to pay attention for a few seconds at least, in order to see if you are worth listening to.

If you do not begin strongly they may decide that you are not worthy of their attention, or that they are not going to be interested in what you have to say, and they will switch off there and then.

We totally disagree with the traditional view that a speaker should warm up the audience with platitudes and obligatory jokes which are rarely relevant. We much prefer a direct, bold beginning, stating what the presentation is going to be about, or bringing forward a key section from the conclusion and then explaining how you got there.

Always try to begin with a quote, an illustrative anecdote or a description of danger, anything that will catch people's attention and hold it. Hopefully the opening anecdote will act as an illustration to the key points you are going to be making later in the presentation. That way you have fixed a picture in the minds of the listeners which they can refer back to as you proceed.

Always beware of jokes. To begin with there are very few people who can tell them successfully, and even if you do manage to raise a laugh, you may be setting the wrong tone for the rest of the presentation. It is unlikely that you really want them to laugh at you or your messages.

Best of all, try to state your key message right at the beginning, while everyone is still listening.

A central theme

As you work through the presentation, make sure that there is one central theme or skeleton, and that you never stray too far away from it.

However good you are as a presenter, there are bound to be moments when people's attention will wander. If you have more than one theme they may be distracted at the moment when you change subjects, and they will then have no idea what you are talking about.

Even more fundamental than that, however, is the danger that the more themes you have the less likely it is that anyone will remember them.

Structuring the message from start to finish

In many cases you could even open your presentation with the punchy message which traditional presenters might leave to the end.

This approach is absolutely consistent with our advice to 'start strong', and will frequently be the easiest way to produce an arresting opener to establish your theme. In most cases your opening and closing lines should state exactly the same key facts or messages, although probably in different formats.

In highly technical industries like engineering and information technology, the culture for presentation-giving is often a direct reflection of how their engineering projects are structured.

They start by collecting a mass of data, which is then massaged through a number of tests until eventually it is distilled down and points them in a particular direction. A drawing then begins to take shape and finally it starts to look like a wing of an aeroplane, a piston for a car or a piece of software.

This is not a good way to create presentations, but it is traditional. All too often this type of presenter starts by saying to the audience 'let me give you the background'.

If, for instance, it is an aviation product, that background might start with the Wright brothers in Kittyhawk, North Carolina, move on through the development of pressurization and the introduction of the jet engine until the speaker finally arrives at the subject which he or she actually wants to talk about – say the recommendation that a turned-

Figure 2

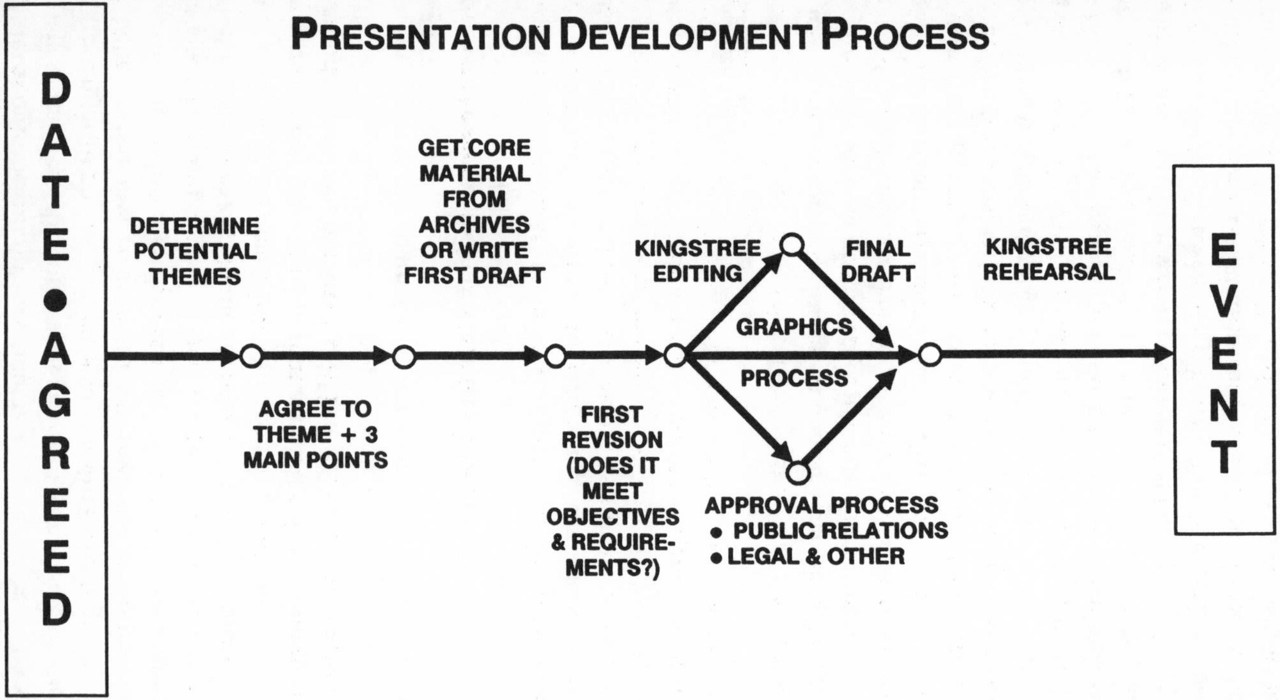

PRESENTATION DEVELOPMENT PROCESS

DATE ● AGREED

DETERMINE
POTENTIAL
THEMES

AGREE TO
THEME + 3
MAIN POINTS

GET CORE
MATERIAL
FROM
ARCHIVES
OR WRITE
FIRST DRAFT

FIRST
REVISION
(DOES IT
MEET
OBJECTIVES
& REQUIRE-
MENTS?)

KINGSTREE
EDITING

GRAPHICS
PROCESS

FINAL
DRAFT

APPROVAL PROCESS
● PUBLIC RELATIONS
● LEGAL & OTHER

KINGSTREE
REHEARSAL

EVENT

up winglet should be put on a particular aircraft rather than extending the wings a few feet, because an extension would mean the planes would no longer fit the airport gateways around the world.

We believe that this is quite the wrong way of approaching the subject, because it violates the principle that one's maximum point of impact is at the start.

We believe the speaker should start by talking about the winglet and why it is needed, and then fill in any necessary background.

If it is done that way the chances are that the presentation will be shorter and more 'receiver-driven', because by starting with the key point the listener has been put on notice of what the message is and given a concrete theme against which to check everything else that the speaker talks about.

With the traditional format the listener is left in suspense as to what the talk is about until the very end, and so has no frame of reference for judging whether the presentation is making sense or not as it proceeds.

So 'start strong'. Produce an arresting, memorable opener to establish your theme.

Turn on the spotlight

Think of a presentation as being like a spotlight, a sharp beam of light illuminating a small area of detail, not a floodlight covering a vast area.

Select a few key points carefully, then illuminate them and bring them alive with colourful, concrete examples.

For every point you make, try to find a metaphor, analogy or anecdote which will illustrate it and link it to the main theme or problem. That way you can build mental pictures in the minds of the audience.

The best way to make a complex concept understandable is to use examples which are familiar to all the listeners, whether they are from the world of work or the every-day world of the family.

This brings us back to our key point about the power of casual conversation to be understandable and memorable. In normal conversation you would make what you were saying as accessible as possible to the person you were talking to. The same theories should apply when you are 'presenting', and only by applying them can you make your words come alive and your personality shine through.

Presidential oratory as conversation

My father once made a six-part record to celebrate the American Bi-centennial. He invited celebrities such as Ronald and Nancy Reagan, Burt Lancaster and Henry Fonda, to enact famous scenes from American history, with American music played by the London Symphony Orchestra and himself doing the narration. Walter Pidgeon played President Lincoln.

When directing the performers he persuaded them all to deliver these pieces, traditionally known either as literary works or oratory, in a conversational style – following the Kingstree presentation rules.

So, when Walter Pidgeon did the Second Inaugural address given after Lincoln had been through the Civil War, he invested it with all the weariness which the President must have felt at the time.

Whereas we tend to think of it as a piece of fine oratory, it is much more likely that Lincoln did actually speak it in a conversational manner, and hearing it presented that way by Walter Pidgeon suddenly brings it alive for the listener in a completely new way.

End dramatically

At the end you need to close dramatically. You should leave people with a call to action, and a summary of all your key points.

If you can finish with an emotional appeal all the better, whether it is to give them hope, fear or pride, anything that will make them think about what you have said in relation to themselves and their own situations. Ending with an inspirational anecdote will help to cement the message in their minds.

Although it is important not to over-rehearse, it is vital to put in at least one rehearsal for any important speech or presentation. The more experienced presenters all know the importance of a 'dress rehearsal'. It is only by simulating the conditions of the actual presentation as closely as possible that you can get any idea how it is going to feel when the adrenalin starts pumping.

Most Kingstree clients rehearse specific speeches in front of us before they go before a real audience, even if they are experienced speakers and highly skilled in using our approach.

That way we can correct any bad habits which they are slipping into, and make absolutely certain that the key points come through when spoken. After all, prior to that run-through all reviewing of the material has probably been visual (reading). No-one has yet spoken those words out loud to test if they sound as good as they look.

Forget the mirror

Under no circumstances should anyone ever rehearse in front of a mirror!

A video camera can help when preparing for an event, but there are still problems if you are taping and reviewing your own remarks. It is really of limited value unless it is being used as part of a professional training and advice session, with a trained advisor who can interpret what appears on the screen for you.

When you video someone, or even take a picture with a still camera, you have immediately edited. By zooming the camera in on the person you have cut out all the background and any distractions which will be there for the live audience, whether it is billowing curtains, other presenters waiting to speak or members of the audience talking, clinking coffee cups or shuffling papers.

The human eye has a wide field of vision and will see much more than just the speaker. A camera, therefore, immediately creates a distortion.

So if you film yourself you will see small things – say you scratched your nose at one point – which will seem like huge movements in a replay. Yet to a live audience scratching your nose would have looked like a small and perfectly natural gesture, in fact they probably would not have noticed it at all.

But because it looked so noticeable to you on the tape, you see it as a potential distraction and so vow not to do it. Immediately you do that you are forcing yourself to behave in an unnatural way, and you have given yourself something to worry about when you should be concentrating on presenting your message, and compensating for the effects of the adrenalin.

Using a mirror is even worse because you are having to make judgements about your performance at the same time as you are thinking about giving it. It is impossible to do these two things at once, and anyway by definition you are receiving a distorted picture, a 'mirror image'.

Traditional wisdom says that the more eye contact you have with the audience the better. We would disagree with that in part, but we would agree that a natural amount of eye contact is good.

The reason it is good is that it gives you a chance to see what is happening amongst your audience, to see if they are still with you, to make it a two-way communication and to make it receiver-driven.

So what sort of feedback are you going to get if you stare into your own eyes in the mirror? You certainly won't see someone else reacting to your ideas. I can see no value in talking a message into a mirror, staring at the guy who's delivering the message – it seems bizarre to us but some industry 'experts' will advise you to do it.

Writing memorable and persuasive speeches

The structure of a presentation, therefore, will be largely determined at the writing stage. That may mean writing a complete script, or simply preparing notes. It doesn't matter which form you choose, as long as you allow enough time for the thought processes needed to identify, clarify and illustrate your key points.

When it comes to speech-writing we are back in an area where we run headlong into established literary traditions.

Writing speak-language

When a senior executive asks a company speech-writer to go away and write something for him, the speech-writer is likely to come back with something which is a grammatically perfect piece of prose. It will flow before the eye and will contain no mistakes. It will not, however, be conversational. It will therefore not sound natural when delivered because no-one talks in beautifully crafted literary sentences.

Even if the speech-writer knows this, however, and writes the speak-language for the boss, the chances are that when he hands his work in the boss, or worse the boss's well-intentioned secretary, will start correcting the grammar, finishing the sentences, cutting out repetitions, and turning the whole thing into something which would make a good article for a magazine but a totally unsuitable presentation.

We work with a number of our clients to help them over this hurdle. They send us the speeches which they have written or had written for them, and we then convert them to suit their own personal, conversational style.

It is an interesting exercise to read some of the published texts of naturalistic modern plays. If you read them on the page it often takes a few seconds to grasp what they are saying because the lines are written to be spoken not to be read.

Speeches should be approached in the same way. Playwrights know how to make dialogues and monologues sound convincing. Many traditional speech-writers do not.

The flow of the sentences, and the words that are used, must come naturally to the speaker, otherwise it will be impossible for him to talk in the same way as he does in normal conversation. Someone with a strong regional accent must be able to talk in a normal voice, and must not be given a speech which was prepared with a completely different speaker in mind.

The same is true of the content. Some people are naturally humorous, others are more serious. While it is important to find a method of delivery which will put the key messages across as forcefully as possible, they cannot be couched in ways with which the presenter feels unhappy.

If in doubt – shorten

In the vast majority of cases speeches are too long, and generally take far too many pages to come to the point. They often contain too many points for an audience to be able to remember.

Communicating with the speech-writers

Many of the theories which we put forward for effective speech-writing are irrelevant to senior executives and politicians because they delegate all that to their teams of full-time script-writers.

We believe that it is a mistake to delegate too much of the work. Other people can do the research and can prepare scripts, if that is what you need, but they cannot necessarily identify the key messages which you want to put across.

If the speech-writers are given the power to create the messages, they will also have the power to make the executives in question come across effectively or not. It would be foolish for any presenter to hand over the whole job to someone else unless they know each other pretty well, but that is often what happens.

Some years ago we developed a service aimed at improving the skills of corporate speech-writers. One of our first customers for this service was one of the world's largest international oil companies.

We arranged to put on the four-day seminar for six of the corporate speech-writers, who ranged in experience from writing for major political figures, through long periods in journalism to virtual newcomers.

We convened the group for drinks and dinner the night before the seminar started, and walked into the most astonishing atmosphere of hostility.

After a few drinks it emerged that they all took great pride in their ability to write effectively and resented us being brought in to teach them how to do it better.

We managed to convince them that was not what we were there to do, and that we fully appreciated the skills which they had. As we

Figure 3

PRESENTATION DEVELOPMENT PROCESS

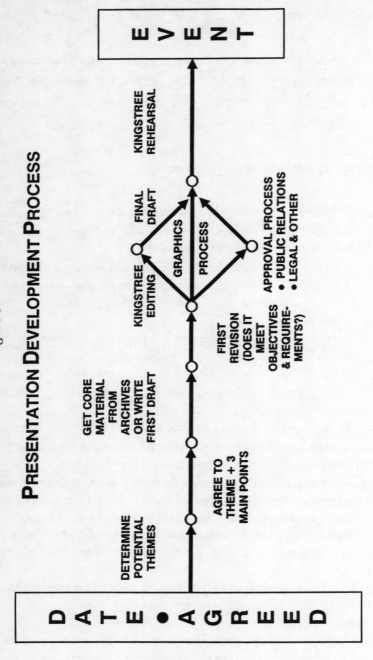

talked, it further emerged that they were bitter because they received absolutely no guidance from the speakers they were writing for about what key points they wanted to make.

These writers, who were allowed to put words into the mouths of the most senior company executives, were not even allowed to meet the speakers to discuss the assignments, and they were kept completely in the dark as to whether or not anything they wrote was ever actually used, either partially or entirely.

The reason for this was the rigidity of the hierarchy in this particular company. The people in the speech-writing team were considered to be so junior in the organization that it was not seen to be appropriate for them to be communicating with the top directors.

The results were that the directors were not getting the sort of support that they deserved, the writers were not able to do their work as well as they were capable of, and the whole process was frustrated for the most ridiculous reasons.

After the seminar we were able to go to the top executives with the speech-writers' case. We explained how vital it was that the creation of presentation material should be seen as a team effort, and that the effort should start with the actual presenters deciding on their key points themselves, and agreeing them right at the beginning, so that their writers had a clear set of instructions to work to.

Then, as the process evolved and drafts were created, we explained, it was quite reasonable for the presenters themselves to review those drafts and make any adjustments necessary.

By doing it that way, whatever the speech-writers created would be built on the core thoughts of the presenters themselves.

The following chart illustrates the presentation development process we use, with the vital 'agreement to theme and main points' occurring as soon as possible after the engagement is confirmed.

The Kingstree presentation strategy

1. BEGIN STRONGLY
(a) Your opening is your point of maximum impact, so don't waste it.

(b) Begin with a quote, illustrative anecdote or description of danger which will catch the audience's attention and relate to their own experiences.

(c) Beware of jokes – they often set the wrong tone.

2. ONE THEME

(a) All presentations should have a central theme or skeleton.

(b) Try writing the close of the speech first – what is the message that you want the audience to take away?

(c) A presentation is like a spotlight (a focused, intense light covering a small area).

(d) Resist trying to cover too many points.

3. CONVERSATIONAL TONE

(a) Beware of written language which is designed to read well.

(b) Use lots of dashes or dots, and broken sentences. Use conversational language.

(c) Don't write sentences which are unnatural to the way you talk – or too long. Short, snappy sentences equal short, snappy thoughts.

(d) Use contractions, e.g. 'we're', rather than 'we are'.

(e) Avoid weak, literary words like 'however'. Use strong alternatives like 'but'.

4. ANALOGY

(a) Find metaphors, analogies or anecdotes to illustrate your main theme or the problems you are addressing.

(b) Use familiar examples to illustrate complex concepts.

5. CLOSE DRAMATICALLY

(a) Close with a call to action.

(b) Summarize the key points.

(c) End with an appeal to emotion such as hope, fear or pride.

(d) End with an inspirational anecdote.

KEY POINTS

- Always prepare key messages
- Be sure you understand your material
- Do not 'learn it'
- Do not over-rehearse
- Start and end strong
- Have a central theme
- Spotlight your key messages
- Always illustrate with anecdotes, metaphors and analogies
- Dress-rehearse in front of an audience
- Write in speak-language
- The messages must be your own

Part II:
Building Personal Influencing Skills

· 14 ·

How to Build Your Self-Confidence

Talking to people, and especially to people we hardly know, can be one of the most daunting things that can happen to any of us. Naturally we all have different levels of confidence. Some of us will only ever feel completely confident when talking to family and close friends, others will be quite happy talking to their peer group around the boardroom table in an informal way.

Everyone, however, finds it difficult to stand up and talk at one level or another. Even the seemingly super-confident chairman of the board will be nervous before the Annual General Meeting or when talking to a journalist on television, and someone who is brilliant on a conference platform may be painfully shy when it comes to talking one-to-one with people at a social function, or when trying to get to know a specific individual of the opposite sex.

One of the main reasons why people seek training to improve their presentation skills is because they want to overcome the nervous tension which they feel when asked to stand up and speak. They believe that if they can just overcome, or control, their nerves, they will then be able to become more effective speakers. In many ways they are right. Even though there is more to effective speaking than self-confidence, it is certainly an excellent starting point.

Self-confidence is a fast-spreading virus; as you become confident in one part of your life, so you will find it rubs off in other areas.

The first thing to recognize is that everyone gets nervous before they make presentations, just as every actor gets nervous before going on stage. Without the nervous tension it would be difficult, if not impossible, to give a good performance. Looked at another way it is safe to say that anyone who is totally confident as he or she walks out onto a stage is bound to be ineffective.

We cannot hope to eradicate those nerves, and in fact we would be doing our clients a disservice if we did. But we can help them to control their anxiety and make the nervous tension easier to live with. And by helping them to be better at making presentations, we can increase their self-confidence in other ways.

Firstly, your confidence will increase because nothing boosts morale as much as conquering fear and excelling at something which previously intimidated you. Secondly, the skills which we develop in clients reflect on every aspect of their dealings with other people.

While a little nervous tension is good for most performances, and adds excitement for ourselves and our audiences, too much can make public speaking such a nightmare for some people that they waste days worrying about forthcoming speaking engagements which should only take up a few hours of preparation time.

They work to get every detail of their script perfect, and spend sleepless nights wondering whether they will be heckled and booed from the stage.

Of course in reality such extremes seldom happen. However frightened the speaker may be, most non-political speeches, particularly badly-presented ones, pass by their audiences with barely a ripple. However, by making sure absolutely nothing can go awry, nervous speakers drain all life and electricity from their presentations. In their anxiety to do nothing wrong, they end up taking no risks and giving bland, uninspiring speeches.

They will have succeeded in not being booed off the stage, but they will have failed to make an effective presentation. They may have escaped the embarrassment of a forgotten line or the exposure of an incorrect fact, but they have completely missed all the opportunities for putting across their messages and impressing themselves on people's memories.

By demonstrating to our clients the enormous gap between how they feel and how the audience feels, caused by the adrenalin pumping through their systems, we can also demonstrate how little it will matter if they stumble over their words, lose their place or say something ungrammatical. We can show them that that is how people talk in normal conversation, and that that is how they successfully put across their personalities without having to think about what they are doing.

Once they realize how little these things actually matter, their fears will decrease and suddenly they won't be making the errors any more – or at least they won't notice them, which comes to the same thing.

If you are nervous a few seconds spent searching for a right word can seem like an eternity to you. But to the audience it will be barely noticeable – if it is noticeable it will look like a pause for thought, which is something positive.

Overcoming the fear of failure

Virtually everyone knows, in his heart of hearts, of at least one major opportunity which was missed simply because he was afraid to try.

He may have told himself that there was no point in going for whatever it was because he had no hope of winning, but in reality it was probably a fear of failure which held him back.

When it comes to presenting, fear of failure is an enormous hurdle. It makes people avoid having to speak at all, and when they can't avoid it they don't make any impact because they dare not take any risks.

It happens to all of us. Whenever we stand up in front of a group of people and begin to talk we are obsessed with what the audience thinks of us, when in reality they are not thinking about us nearly as much as we imagine.

The same applies in selling and new business pitching situations: people decide not to run at all rather than be seen to try and fail. Yet trying and failing is the best possible learning experience.

By providing people with a technique which they can rely on not to let them down, we give them the courage to take a few more risks.

Once they have mastered our basic communication techniques and seen the effect our principles have on the audiences they are addressing, they begin to seek out further opportunities to use their new-found speaking skills, and all their horizons broaden as a result.

The more challenges they take on, the more practised and proficient they grow, and it has a snowball effect, the so-called 'virtuous circle'.

The only way to increase self-confidence is to face up to challenges, be daring and excel. Public speaking is a challenge for everyone, but to excel at it you need to master the basic techniques and then practise them relentlessly.

Daring to be yourself

One of the keys to self-confidence is being able to be yourself, and not feeling that you should change to suit other people's expectations.

One of the founding theories of our approach is that people should always be themselves, and should merely work towards projecting that genuine personality more effectively, more consistently and with the minimum time committed to preparation.

One of our clients is a world leader in the detergent business. The company's chief executive is a striking-looking man. Had someone rung Central Casting and asked them to send along an actor who looked the part of a distinguished chief executive, they couldn't have come up with anyone who looked more suited to the role.

He was also an exceptionally formal man, the sort who would keep his suit jacket on all day, and would keep his desk immaculately bare.

The company's corporate communications people decided that it was time for an image-change. They thought it would be a good idea if, when speaking to groups of headquarters staff, the chief executive sat on the edge of his desk, took his jacket off and 'rapped' with his audience. They asked us to convince him that this would be a good thing to do.

I knew that if we suggested he should do this, the chief executive would take our advice, because he was a very effective delegator, and he trusted us. But I warned the communications team that they would be asking for trouble.

Firstly he would feel uncomfortable because it was not his style, and anyone in the audience who knew him well would be distracted from the key messages by this extraordinary change in personality.

If he did manage to carry it off, however, there was a risk that people sitting in the audience would get completely the wrong impression of the sort of man he was.

They would then be in for a big shock if they were called in to see him because of some problem. They might go into the meeting thinking they were in for a cosy fireside chat, but by the end they were going to feel as if they had backed into an airplane propeller.

If a chief executive, or any senior executive, starts giving out contradictory signals like that, he is going to end up with a confused and worried staff.

If people are given the confidence to be themselves, then they can handle almost any problem on their own terms.

If they start pretending that they are someone else, they will soon either show their true colours, or lose their confidence in what is the appropriate reaction to any given situation.

Giving confidence to a start-up business

Some of our clients come to us because we have worked with their companies in the past and they then go out and form start-up businesses elsewhere.

In this situation people often lack confidence because of their lack of track record. They feel unable to compete effectively with firms which have been established for many years.

What we have to tell them is that, in most cases, customers hire people, not companies. They want to know if the people who are talking to them are going to be able to help them solve some problem or other.

If our clients can just put across their personalities, ideas and skills, the potential client will listen to what they have to say.

If they are competent enough at what they do to feel that they can build a company on their own talents, and if their potential client is sufficiently confident of their abilities to have asked them to pitch for the business at all, then they have a fair chance of winning whatever work they go after.

It is possible that they will lose some pitches because of size, when the client prefers a company which can offer a strong back-up or international network, but it is just as likely that they will win some business from clients who are trying to get away from the big company mentality, and who want a more personal service.

The key issue is for the principals of the new business to focus their minds on what they can do for the client, and then put the key points clearly to the buying panel or executive. They need to do the best possible job of listening to what the customer wants, and of asking intelligent questions, so that they can establish a personal dialogue which will make it irrelevant whether they have been in business for six months or 60 years.

Increasing your earning power

All too often the people who earn the most money are simply the ones who have the confidence to ask for it. The same people also have the ability to project their personalities and their abilities to others in their own company or industry. They get noticed, their achievements are recognized and they are rewarded for those achievements.

There is always a tendency to measure people by their own standards. If you don't seem confident of your own abilities most people will assume that you have nothing to be confident about.

In virtually any profession, anyone who wants to get to the top will have to master the arts of spoken communication and presentation-giving. At every level of the management ladder it is vital to be able to communicate effectively with others in order to sell yourself, your services, your products and your ideas.

It doesn't matter how good you are at your job if nobody knows about you. So it is vital to be able to project your personality in order to be remembered by the people that matter, and to communicate your ideas effectively if you want to influence the events which go on around you.

If you are able to communicate skilfully you will be able to put yourself across effectively at job interviews and salary reviews, and you will be able to explain yourself and your actions to your bosses as you progress through your career.

You will become known as someone who 'knows his subject' and 'gets things done', and everyone needs to hire people with those characteristics.

If you believe you should be earning more, or handling a more challenging and interesting workload, you need to be able to explain what it is you want to do and why. That can only happen if you are confident of your abilities, and of your spoken communications skills.

By mastering the skills for use in business presentation settings, it is possible to use them in every aspect of your life.

Attracting sponsorship

Many of our clients sponsor sports people and athletes, or use well-known individuals as part of their promotional plans. It can provide a large source of revenue to the sponsored individuals, but they have to be able to provide value for money to the client.

That generally means that the clients expect the athletes to speak in public on their behalf, and to give media interviews. Those who have reached the top in the sports world are not necessarily skilled public speakers, and we are often called in to help them become more confident, and consequently more useful to the sponsoring company.

Unless the chosen spokespeople are effective at personal communications it will reflect badly on the company, and that will mean that the sponsorship money may be diluted or wasted.

KEY POINTS

- Nerves are necessary
- Control is possible
- Self-confidence snowballs
- Understand the effects of adrenalin
- Failing is a positive learning experience
- Be yourself
- Let people know your worth

· 15 ·

Using the Approach in Other Walks of Life

University applications

For many people, applying for a place at a university may be the first time they find themselves in a formal interview. They need, therefore, to do some preparation beforehand.

If they can, they should get some professional help, but obviously that is not available to everyone. The next best thing is to read books like this one, and consider deeply what approach to take and, if a willing friend can be found, to role-play and rehearse the way things are likely to go.

The most important thing which they can do is focus themselves on the communication from the recipients' point of view. What, they must ask themselves, are these people looking for?

The answer is that they are trying to see the interviewee's real personality. They are looking for a sense of curiosity and commitment. So the interviewees must work out how they can best put those qualities across.

Because it is a first experience, the interviewee may not be aware of just how the stress and adrenalin will affect him or her. It is hard to simulate the experience without the help of professionals, but not impossible.

Job interviews

The next hurdle for many people is the first job interview, and there has been a great deal of material written over the years advising people on how to behave.

The same basic rules apply as in any other presenting situation. You need to decide what the listener is looking for, and then work out the best way of establishing that you can provide it.

In some cases it will be inappropriate to take any form of notes with you into a job interview except possibly to refer to when the interviewer asks if you have any questions. Certainly this is one area where you must be seen to be ad-libbing.

At some points, however, it is quite legitimate to use notes during an interview. If, for instance, the interviewer asks you to run through your previous work history, you could refer to your c.v., to make sure you don't miss anything out. You can then take out some previously prepared notes on your employment history and use them just as you would if making a speech or speaking to a meeting:

Glance down, pick up a fact, make eye contact, pause for thought and then speak. Pause again to check that it has registered and glance down again, and so on.

Here you have a real opportunity to make the message receiver-driven, which you might not have if you were standing up on a stage giving a speech. For instance, as you deliver each point the interviewer might be taking notes, in which case you can slow your delivery to match the rate of writing. If he or she is just listening then you will get very clear signals as to whether you should continue to talk, or whether you have said enough.

Interviewers will also be able to interject questions if they want you to elaborate on any particular point.

It is important that you allow them to dictate the pace in this way, although you must not let them deter you from stressing the key points of your message.

By setting the pace of the interview in this way, it will be easier to maintain it during the less structured parts, where the interviewer will be asking questions which you may not be expecting, and where you will have to answer off the top of your head.

Whenever you are asked a question, take as long as you need to think of the answer. While you are thinking remain silent and do not try to cover the silence with waffle . . . e.g. Oh, well, I don't know, let's think, I suppose if I were honest, ummm . . . You will not be able to think clearly if you are talking like this and you will seem flustered rather than thoughtful.

It would be a good idea to prepare yourself before the interview, as you would with a formal presentation, making a list of the key messages that you want to get across. It might be your experience in a particular industry, your keenness to move into a new area, or a particular skill you have acquired in a previous job.

Whatever these messages are, writing them down will help to clarify them in your mind, and will make them more readily available to you when you are asked questions such as 'why do you want this job?' or 'why do you think you could do this job?'

It would also be worth jotting down all the likely questions which an interviewer might ask, and thinking through your answers.

It would be a mistake to write your responses out in full, because then you might be tempted to try to remember them word-for-word, leading to panic if you are unable to do so. But if you take the time to think through exactly what your opinions are before getting there, you are less likely to give half-baked answers.

Another key to success in job interviews is to have done your homework on the company to which you are applying. Ideally your research will allow you to draw up a list of questions you can ask the interviewer.

Topics for probing questions might include recent events or changes in the industry, how the company sees its competitive strength against others in the sector, recent changes in management or ownership, movement of stock price or virtually anything else which will allow the interviewer to see that you have taken the trouble to prepare.

Being prepared to ask a few considered, open-ended questions also forces the interviewer to give you his or her views on the subjects you have raised, and might well create openings for you to comment, and further demonstrate your depth and commitment. Avoid asking closed questions which could elicit a simple 'yes' or 'no' approach. The objective is to get the interviewer to talk.

The legal profession

We have worked extensively in the world of corporate law, not just for the lawyers themselves, who need to be able to persuade and influence people to their point of view all the time, but also for corporations who need to provide expert witnesses who can put their messages across clearly and memorably in what is often major litigation.

The need for clear and memorable spoken communications is probably better illustrated in a complex court case than in almost any other arena. If judges and juries are not clear about the key issues facing them, then they can't hope to make balanced decisions. If lawyers are not able to put across their cases in sensible, persuasive ways, they will not be successful.

Many of the most successful people in the legal profession are brilliant spoken communicators, but frequently these successful people don't really know how they manage to achieve it. If they were taught how to control their abilities and channel them more forcefully, they could increase their powers a hundredfold by being consistent and avoiding the occasional 'off-day' which plagues athletes and others who suceed by natural ability rather than by learnt behaviour.

Most lawyers understand this, yet they frequently confuse clients, colleagues, jurors and others by describing complicated events or concepts in convoluted and arcane language. It is easy to observe in the law a direct parallel with the high technology industries. At the root of the problem is a failure to keep it simple and to use concrete examples to illustrate abstract concepts.

Once again it is a failure on the part of the presenters to take into account the needs of the recipients of the message. The legal profession is very apt to lapse into jargon and inflated 'professional-speak', which leaves normal people scrabbling to make sense of what they are hearing and trying to translate it into everyday language.

The academic sector

When we are at school, most of us are led to believe that if we are unable to remember what our teachers say, or if our concentration wanders while they are talking, it is in some way our fault.

In reality the exact opposite is true. It is the teacher's job to hold our attention and ensure that the key messages get across to us and are memorable.

Many of us spend time teaching and lecturing at some stages of our lives, even if we don't make a career out of it. It is an activity which can provide enormous satisfactions and where it is possible to make a genuine difference to other people's lives – but only if we communicate effectively.

There is a massive gap between what goes on in the academic sectors of western society and what goes on in the real world.

The whole communication dynamic is turned on its head because in the world of education the people who are receiving the information usually have to pass an exam on what has been said. That very rarely happens in the real world, where it is the speaker who is the one on trial rather than the listeners.

Because certain amounts of information have to be got through within certain time-frames in order to keep to a syllabus, the information imparted in an educational course is bound to be transmitter-driven rather than receiver-driven, as it should be in every other spoken communication situation.

Having said that, a teacher whose students do not pass their exams is very soon going to be out of a job, so good teachers are likely to be interested in anything they can do to improve the retention rate of their students.

By using the same techniques we have described for the business world, teachers can increase the visual imagery and colour of their lessons, and can ensure that they are taking into account the needs of the receivers of information in order to maximize the amounts of material which they are able to absorb successfully.

Many good teachers do the things which we are recommending, but they are good communicators instinctively. They know they are successful but they don't necessarily know why. If these people actually stopped to analyse what it is that they are doing right, they could increase the power of their teaching skills overnight.

Using the skills of a tutor

To some degree the way in which people in the outside world give presentations is a reflection of what goes on in our schools and universities.

In the lecture format the speaker assumes that the class will have to keep up with the flow of ideas and information if they want to pass their exams. So the pace of communication is governed by the syllabus and the amount of material which has to be covered in a given time, making it entirely transmitter-driven.

In a tutorial, however, the educational material is delivered at the speed at which the student can absorb it. If at a tutorial the instructor senses that the individual hasn't understood something, then it is possible to go back and spend as much time as necessary before moving, on. Likewise if the pupil is absorbing the information quickly the instructor can move on sooner.

The tutorial, therefore, is obviously a great deal more efficient in terms of the time spent by the student, but it requires one-to-one contact which is not always possible.

What we are saying, however, is that a good presentation should be a reflection of what goes on in a tutorial as opposed to what goes on in the lecture hall. All too often, presenters talking to groups of people operate as if the same dynamics were at work as in the university – but their audiences do not have to listen. Even professional conference organizers add to the problem by inviting their speakers to talk for 30 or sometimes 45 minutes, exceeding the average listener's attention span by 50-100 per cent.

KEY POINTS

- Focus on the recipient's viewpoint
- Prepare thoroughly for every presenting situation
- Be comfortable with silence
- Most audiences have the option of not listening

· 16 ·

Internal Meetings and Presentations

Whether we like them or loathe them, internal meetings are the driving force behind most organizations. When teamwork is important to success, people need to know what other team members are thinking and doing, and they need to reach conclusions on what actions to take based on the combined knowledge and opinions of the team.

People who are not good at communicating ideas in the setting of a meeting room will not be able to make much of a contribution to the team effort. They will also be frustrated in their jobs because they will constantly see other people's wishes and ideas being carried out before and against their own.

In meetings, most people are more interested in what they themselves are saying than what anyone else has to contribute. They are either waiting their turn to speak, and mentally rehearsing their views, or they are thinking about what they have just said and wondering if they could have done it better.

What they are not doing is listening to you. You have to make them do that. To start with, you must stick to the point, because the moment people think you are waffling or wandering off-track they will tune out or interrupt you. That is where the use of notes comes in.

Secondly you must catch their attention, and this can be done with the use of visual imagery – giving them mental pictures which they can relate to their own experiences – and through silence.

If you start to speak and have managed to catch the attention of the others, or if you have been asked a question and all eyes are on you, awaiting your answer, the longer you pause the greater the anticipation will be amongst the listeners. Those who were not paying attention will have their interest caught by an unexpected silence; and those who are listening will be impressed by your confidence and by the obvious thought which you are putting into your words.

Just as when you are speaking on a more formal occasion, you need to allow pauses for people to think about what you have said. When you are on a platform, however, the chances are that no-one will interrupt you or assume you have finished speaking. At an informal meeting, where everything is relatively relaxed and everyone has an individual agenda to work to, you will need to make sure that people are aware the pauses are deliberate and that they do not see them as opportunities for other people to butt in.

One way of achieving that is with eye contact. After you have made your point, and you are pausing to give them time to understand it, look them in the eye, asking for a response to show that they have understood what you have said and that they are happy for you to move on. If you don't use eye contact boldly at these stages you will find yourself 'talked over' by someone bolder or more experienced.

It doesn't matter how casual a meeting it is, it always pays to prepare. It also saves time in the long run. If you have regular morning meetings with other departments for instance, it is worth spending five minutes the night before, or first thing in the morning, jotting down the things you want to talk about. If you go in unprepared and just talk off the top of your head you will waste much more of your own time and the others won't be as likely to listen: your efforts will be wasted and you will have missed an opportunity.

Running successful meetings

All the theories which we use to allow people to make more effective presentations, also work for improving the way meetings are run.

Points can be made more forcefully, time can be saved and decisions can be reached more effectively, if certain disciplines are adhered to.

One of our major customers is divided into two major divisions. Once a month the senior managers of one or other of those divisions goes to the company's headquarters to make a report.

When we were introduced to the company, each of the meetings was scheduled to take four and a half hours, and each time they found that they still weren't covering everything that was on the agenda.

This was in spite of the fact that the lead-time for ordering a product in this company could be as long as four or five years.

It didn't seem possible that with such product lead-times and planning cycles, they could justify spending four and a half hours every 60 days talking about what had changed since the last meeting.

How much could possibly have happened during that time, that they had to bore everybody to distraction by talking about it?

As we went deeper into it, we found that the system had evolved because the company had held such a pre-eminent position in its industry for so long. Over the years they had found it easy to sit around and talk about details for hours because, firstly, all the people at the top of the company had engineering backgrounds, and secondly, they had very little else to do because there was virtually no effective competition.

There was also another cultural issue. People in the organization had come to believe that the longer they held the floor, the more their visibility or profile was enhanced. Rather than a culture that rewarded a brief and concise approach, the reverse had evolved.

I suggested to the head of one of the divisions that he should start the next meeting by saying something along the lines of; Gentlemen, there is not much news since we were here last, but there are two or three things we would like to talk about; Jones is going to cover 'A', Smith is going to cover 'B', and then I would like to wrap it up with a few comments about 'C'.

That immediately put the executives from head office on notice about what that divisional head thought was important that day, and they were able to cut the meetings down to an hour and a half instead of the original four and a half hours.

Each speaker could then summarize the key points he or she was going to cover, and if the head office executives had no questions they could move straight on to the next topic. If there were questions, they found that they seldom needed more than 20 minutes to deal with them.

From the point of view of the head office executives, it meant that not only were they able to get the meeting over in a third of the time, they were also being given hard information which was actually useful. In the past they had come away from the meetings with a mass of data which they had to sift in order to find the key issues – another big saving in time.

The same principles apply to any meeting. All too often people go in with no idea what they are going to talk about, and the conversation 'evolves' round to the most important subjects.

If each person arrived with a few key points to put across or discuss, and stated them clearly at the outset, the amount of time needed for each meeting would be cut to the bone.

Annual general meetings

For senior management the AGM probably represents the more formal end of the business speaking disciplines. In many cases this is the one time of the year that the shareholders of all sizes get a good look at the board of directors in whose hands their prosperity lies.

Yet it is probably one of the tasks which fewest senior executives prepare for adequately. Maybe they feel that having successfully run large companies all year, many with subsidiaries all round the world, and because they have been successful at running meetings in all these companies all through the year, they will be perfectly well equipped to run a good AGM with very little effort.

In reality there is much more to it than they might suppose.

It is very important that they get over the key messages of the company to the assembled audience, some of whom, such as financial journalists and analysts, will be passing the information on to wider audiences. They should be seen to be doing a professional job because it is the only time that most of them will actually be seen at work by these crucial audiences. If they perform badly at the AGM the audience can only assume that they perform equally badly at other times.

They must be well briefed on likely questions and have their answers fully prepared, since it may well be the spontaneous question from a member of the audience which ends up being quoted in the press. If that is the one question that they failed to answer satisfactorily then that is the total impression which readers of the media will receive.

There will normally be employees present at an AGM, perhaps because they too are shareholders, and they need to be given confidence that their leaders know what they are doing and are taking the company in the right directions.

At some AGMs there may even be professional hecklers sent in to ask awkward questions, and they need to be handled carefully. The person taking the questions needs to be able to keep the sympathy of the audience while putting down the heckler.

He or she also needs to know how to delegate questions out to other members of the team, further demonstrating that they are the right people to be trusted with control of the company.

Although the AGM provides a valuable opportunity for senior management to put across some key messages, this is one situation where they can break some of the cardinal rules of presentation. One of the main purposes of these events is to send audiences away with warm feelings about the company in question. If there aren't any key messages to be put across, then it will be enough if everyone feels confident that the company is going up not down, that its fate is in safe hands, and that there is no need to worry for the coming year.

That means that you can use visual aids like company videos and slide shows, without worrying whether their messages are memorable or whether they are distracting from the speakers' main points.

This situation changes radically, of course, if the company is going through a bad time, or if there is a stated lack of confidence in the management. Under those circumstances it is crucial that the board takes firm control of the messages and ensures that everyone goes away knowing what is being done to put things right.

KEY POINTS

- You have to *make* people listen
- Meetings need structure and key points
- Use eye contact to maintain control
- Start your contribution to any meeting with something crisp and succinct

· 17 ·

Taking to the Conference Platform

For many people a major company conference is the first time they have to face really large audiences. Those who are successful at internal conference speaking, however, can go on to make an impact at industry conferences and other events which can boost their own reputations and the reputations of their companies.

Conference platforms can provide effective speakers with unrivalled opportunities to put messages across to target audiences, including the media. They also provide opportunities for endless streams of dull and unmemorable presentations.

In many cases there will be professional production companies involved in the staging of large-scale shows, and their job will be to provide all the necessary facilities to back you up.

The important thing is to remain in control of your segment, and not to let the production team swamp your message with overly dramatic audiovisual effects which can distract the audience if they don't really serve to illustrate your specific points.

If you are not happy about anything they are doing in your segment, speak up. The organizers or producers may have good reasons why they have to do what they have planned, but they may also be quite agreeable to change things to fit in with your ideas and requirements.

You may also be asked to provide a transcript of your speech in advance, so that the organizers can publish it and give it to delegates at the end, or distribute to the media. If this happens make sure that you prepare two versions, one to be read and one to be spoken. Remember that if you read aloud the one which has been written with a view to being published you will sound stilted and dull, and you will not be able to get your points across as readily, because the language is too literary in style.

If the conference involves a number of different speakers, they will need to know exactly how long you are going to speak for, so that they can schedule everyone else around you. The difficulty for inexperienced speakers is knowing how long they will actually be talking.

Very few people have a sense of how much material they can cover in a finite amount of time. Most assume that in the 15 or 20 minutes that they have been allotted, they will be able to put in a lot more data than is actually possible.

What we invariably find is that when clients either send us material that they propose to deliver, or come in to rehearse something with us, we have to make as much as a 50 per cent cut in length.

The only way to become skilled at this is practice, but if you start by opening with a key point and then illustrating that key point with a few concrete examples, it is surprising how easy it is to keep the presentation simpler than might otherwise be possible.

When making the notes – or writing out the speech in full – bear in mind that it can be divided into time segments. If you have three key points to make in 15 minutes, you know that you have five minutes for each of them.

As you pause to look at your notes, check that you are not running ahead of or behind your timings. Taking those few extra seconds to check the time and see if you are on course will also help you to prolong the pauses which the adrenalin is trying to shorten all the time.

Never worry about taking the time to look at a clock or your watch, (not with an obvious movement which the audience can see), and check if you are on target. It will never take more than a few seconds and will rarely be noticeable to the audience.

As noted earlier, the maximum length of time that most audiences can concentrate on one speaker is 18 minutes. Many conference organizers, however, allow 45 minutes per speaker. If that is the case then you should aim to talk for as little over 20 minutes as possible, and let the organizers know that is what you plan to do. This may seem discourteous: but ask yourself when was the last time you were in an audience and honestly felt that the speaker had been too brief?

If it is a large conference there will probably be a panel discussion after every couple of speakers. If it is a smaller show the microphone may be passed around for questions after each speech. In either case the chairman will be quite happy to have a speaker finish early and provide a little leeway, because most people will make the mistake of saying too much and over-running their time.

Someone who is invited to speak at a conference needs to start preparing several weeks in advance. You must first decide what presentation tool you are going to use – script or notes. For a formal situation that will normally mean a full script.

The script must then be written in 'speak-language', with a strong start, key messages and a punchy end. Whoever writes the speech, whether it is the speaker, a professional speech-writer or a public relations company, it must always be translated into 'speak-language' if it is to sound natural.

KEY POINTS

- Use conference platforms to set your own agenda
- Remain in total control of your slot
- Know how long you have and cut your message to fit the audience's attention span
- Divide your material into time segments
- Remember to write in 'speak-language'

· 18 ·

Improving Your Social Skills

Although we have stated very firmly that people communicate at their best in casual conversation, there are many people who find certain social situations almost as daunting as standing up on a stage and speaking to an audience.

Meeting strangers for the first time or going to parties can fill some highly able and intelligent people with untold fears.

Anyone who has felt those fears and who has had any experience of life, will know that on the whole they are illogical. In their hearts most people know that strangers met at parties are usually anything but hostile, but the fears will persist.

In the main those fears centre around the worry that you will not be able to think of anything to say, or that you will not be able to understand what other people are talking about. They are, on the whole, all about being confident regarding communication.

If someone has become confident and competent at communicating in any situation, then there is nothing to fear. And, since most people are nervous to some degree in company, those who are trained well will automatically come to dominate most situations which they enter, including social ones.

At any gathering it is always possible to see the people who are the most skilled at communicating; they radiate confidence and charm and, if you take the opportunity to follow them around for a while, you will find they say surprisingly little.

What they are good at is putting other people at their ease, and then listening to and guiding those people as they talk. Often the most socially skilled people are the ones with the fewest original thoughts. Anyone can do it by learning a few basic rules.

The first rule is to maintain the right degree of eye contact. It is no good saying 'Hi, good to see you' to somebody if you are looking over his shoulder to see who else is in the room. That does not mean, however, that you should stare the other person down, unless you have a reason for wanting to intimidate him.

It is then important to make sure the other person does the lion's share of the talking. No-one ever succeeded in putting across a point of view or in persuading people to change their minds about anything by bombarding them with opinions and facts.

First you need to find out what they think and believe already – they may already think the same way you do – then you can make a few key, telling points which they will remember, rather than boring them with endless talk.

When you find yourself in a social situation which makes you nervous, the temptation is to gush, giving out more information than anyone wants or is able to retain. If you can cut back on the talking, and find the right questions to trigger others into talking, even if they seem almost banal, you are more likely to be able to make a favourable impression, and make people willing to listen when you do have something worth saying.

Business gatherings

Many people in business have to attend those semi-social occasions where business people mingle and make contacts. They can be an agony for anyone who is not self-confident, but they can be of enormous benefit in meeting the right people and making yourself known.

One of the hardest things is breaking away from a group of people you are talking to once you feel you have said all that you have to say, and when you want to move on to meet someone else.

The first thing to accept is that this is difficult, and that you are not the only one who has this problem. Then you can begin to think logically about how to deal with it.

It takes considerable confidence, but what you have to do is be quite blunt and say something like, 'I'd love to catch up with you in a moment, but I must just talk to so-and-so,' and move off. There is no right moment, and if you keep waiting for it you will miss the opportunity. The only way to get it right is to practise it.

It is a question of always remaining in control of situations. You can do that by leading the conversation with your questions, making your points clearly, and then explaining what you are doing (e.g. moving on). If you allow other people to gain control you may not be able to put across whatever messages you want to impart, or to find out any information which will be useful to you, and you may get 'stuck' with someone you don't really want to talk to.

Becoming comfortable with silence

It is also important to become confident enough not to feel that you have to fill every silence that comes along.

Say, for instance, that you are at a formal dinner and you find yourself sitting between a deadly serious financial specialist who appears to have no other interests in life, and someone who has just flown into the country and speaks only a few words of English.

What happens if by the time the main course is served you have already asked all the standard questions, but you have received short answers and no feedback from either of them with which you can build a conversation?

The answer is that you must be quite happy to say nothing, be happy with the silence, just listening to other people around the table. Sooner or later someone will say something which will involve you in another conversation and things will progress naturally.

After-dinner speaking

Although an after-dinner speech is a formal presentation, objectives may be different from those of other situations.

For once it may not be so important that people in the audience remember exactly what you have said. The objective is more that they should be amused and possibly enlightened at the same time. You want them to receive a strong impression of what you are like, and a pleasant feeling about you.

In other words your main priority is the projection of your personality rather than any key points or messages.

Even so, a dinner with a lot of influential people attending could be a good opportunity for you to put across some messages, as long as they are not too overtly selling something when the situation is supposed to be more social than business.

The greatest danger for most people when they want to be liked by the audience is joke-telling.

Many of the most prolific after-dinner speakers are in fact extremely good at telling jokes. Some of them are so good at entertaining people that they can charge enormous sums of money. Most of us are not as good as that, and the results can be embarrassing when we attempt it.

That does not mean, however, that you can't keep a subject light and humorous, but it is a mistake to think that audiences always expect to hear jokes. They would much rather not be embarrassed by someone trying unsuccessfully to be a comedian.

It can be especially hard if you are following someone who has had the audience falling about with laughter, not to be tempted to try to compete and keep the mood going. This is really very difficult, and the audience will probably be disappointed. If you remain true to yourself and your planned remarks they will be just as happy with you as they were with the comedian.

Anyone who accepts a request to speak after dinner is likely to have a specialist subject which the other diners want to hear about, and should stick to that subject. Any humour should be connected to anecdotes about the particular field of expertise.

As with more business-like speeches, however, it is still generally advisable to work from notes, since it keeps you on track. And it is no less vital to use pauses to allow stories and opinions to sink in, or to allow time for the audience to be amused and to laugh.

One of the greatest faults of inexperienced after-dinner speakers is that they will work very hard to find amusing material, only to blow it

by not allowing their listeners a chance to enjoy a good laugh before
they move on to the next point.

Sample speech

The following is a speech made by a company chief executive on the
retirement of an employee. Taking what could be a dull string of
compliments and reminiscences, he has found a theme which is
relevant to people in the audience, who will mostly be of a similar age to
the retiree, and by going to the trouble of doing some research, he has
further demonstrated his regard for the man.

*On Monday, 2nd February, 1942, the black-out period ended for the night at
8.06 am . . . the sun was scheduled to rise at 8.38 am . . . the dollar was quoted
over the weekend at 4.02 to the £ . . . in that day's* Times, *National Provincial
Bank was to publish its statutory statement of assests and liabilities as at 31st
December 1941 . . . It was claimed that its affiliates were Coutts and Grindlay
Co Ltd, and its total balance sheet footings amounted to £497m. . . . the
Japanese forces were on the very doorstep of Singapore . . . Arthur Askey,
Tommy Trinder and Edith Evans were on the West End stage . . . the preceding
Saturday Westminster Bank rugby first team had lost 15–0 to the London Fire
Brigade.*

*As the sun duly rose at 8.38 am that Monday morning in 1942, a handsome,
fresh-faced intelligent, well-dressed, young man of great potential, and 16
summers . . . smoking a very large and smelly pipe, rang at the bell of
Westminster Bank's Machine Accountancy School in Threadneedle Street
London . . . yes folks, you have guessed it – it was our illustrious host this
evening, Gordon Reeve.*

*From that day on is history. But . . . I did promise Gordon that I would not
catalogue his career from those annual crime sheets that make up his cardex.*

*Having read his reports in some detail . . . I can quite understand his
concern. Never have I met a more boring collection of eulogy, as year followed
year: 'standard of work very high' . . . 'cannot speak too highly' . . . 'most
enthusiastic' . . . 'an asset to the staff' . . . 'outstanding' . . . and, I might add
. . . it's quite clear that none of the authors of those reports were paying the
slightest concern to providing material for my few words tonight.*

In those days of secret reporting they could have said so much! Where, I asked

*myself, was the record of those illicit weekday visits to London museums . . .
which John Coombs and Gordon used to indulge in during their hard pressed
days in the Joint General Managers Department of Metropolitan Control
West? (We never had time for that fancy sort of learning in Northern Control).
Where, I asked myself, was the record of Gordon's unnatural attraction to
agricultural shows?*

*What is there in those obscure rural functions that produced the ever-willing
volunteer . . . willing to slap NatWest ribbons on bulls and NatWest rosettes on
chickens all over the United Kingdom. Where – in these silent, glowing reports –
is the record of the torment . . . clearly felt by his soul as this man of Croydon . . .
did move in 1958 . . . North of the River Thames . . . to Bishops Stortford in
Essex. How, we wonder, did he take to this missionary work?*

*However, allowing for this disgraceful and altogether familiar lack of
detailed personnel work, the record does reveal peaks in Gordon's high level,
professional career:*

*War-time service in the RAF took him to air-crew training in Canada and
during those war days he met and married Thelma, who we are delighted to have
here tonight.*

*– a succession of challenging branch appointments in and around London –
two Area Directorships at Croydon and Hyde Park; Deputy General Manager
of Management Services Division in 1982.*

*You might think that all that would have kept him busy. But . . . add his
interests in stamp collecting, antiques, gardening, history, motoring, travel, the
bank's Theatre Club, of which he is President, CoSIRA (Council for Small
Industries in Rural Areas) which he has served as an executive board member for
some 12 years . . .*

*Add these to the mix and you get some idea of the rounded man . . . a real
gentleman with a keen yet kindly wit, a twinkle in his eye, and a lively, mellow
sense of fun in all he does.*

*In all this . . . through his career . . . Gordon has been supported
wholeheartedly by Thelma – through thick and thin – and I know well the
massive contribution made by Thelma, not only in support of Gordon, but in
furtherance of the interests of our great bank.*

*Thelma, we thank you for that . . . and for being the delightful person you
are.*

*As a member of the General Management team, Gordon has made a major
contribution during years of rapid change in the banking industry. That
contribution will help materially to . . . carry us forward . . . in the challenging*

years ahead. Gordon, on behalf of the bank, I thank you for your outstanding service.

On behalf of the bank and your very many friends, I thank you for this evening's festivities and wish you and Thelma all good fortune and good health in the many years ahead . . . years, I know which will be full and happy ones.

Gordon, may this very full book of signatures revive memories of a host of friendships – Ladies and Gentlemen, will you join me in toasting the health and happiness of Thelma and Gordon Reeve.

KEY POINTS

- Competence conquers fears
- Don't be frightened to talk less
- Get the right level of eye contact
- Find out about the other person
- Everyone else has the same problems as you
- Always keep control
- Stick to your own subjects
- Beware of jokes

Part III:
Influencing the Influencers

· 19 ·

Presenting Effectively in the Financial Community

Every business needs to raise money. It may be a question of going to the bank for a loan or to a venture capitalist for an equity investment. Or it may be a matter of dealing with all the major institutional shareholders. It might mean large meetings involving thousands of shareholders, small, intimate and powerful meetings in the board-rooms of London, New York and Tokyo, or meetings with one of the world's leading investment banks.

Whatever the situation, the needs of the audiences are the same. They want to know the facts. They need to hear a vision, backed up by experience, and they want to be able to believe that the person talking to them is going to be able to produce the results that are being forecast.

In most cases they will also need detail, but that should be given to them in written form, not in spoken presentations, especially at the outset of negotiations or financial presentations.

Everyone has to put his or her case clearly and convincingly when trying to raise money, whether it is the chairman of a major industrial corporation needing to raise millions, or an individual going to the bank manager for an overdraft of a few thousand.

There are also a number of major conferences at which members of the financial community talk to one another. Speakers at these conferences are people who have developed reputations for being experts in their particular fields and are invited to talk on their subject. Sometimes these subjects are esoteric and arcane, and to make them understandable the speakers have to bring their statistics alive with anecdotes and illustrations.

Members of the financial community also have to make presentations within the daily routine of their business. Stockbrokers have to tell clients how their portfolios are doing, banks have to talk to customers either one-to-one or in groups, and they all have to win new business, like any other corporations.

Avoid being numbers-driven

The mistake which many people make when presenting information to groups such as financial analysts and investors is to make them 'numbers-driven', in the mistaken belief that the analysts' primary goal is to see a lot of statistics in agonizing detail, with endless forecasts and all the rest of the material which computers can turn out.

But if we actually stop to think what colours and influences the investment decisions and recommendations of the various financial audiences, it will often be their subjective evaluations of the abilities of the management of the company which is presenting its case to them.

They want to see if the managers are capable of dealing with a deteriorating market, for instance, or if they are the sort of people who can take a small company and make it grow.

That does not mean that there should be no figures or forecasts in a presentation. But the figures displayed should be used to illustrate or prove the key points which managers hope to make; they are not themselves the key points.

All too frequently financial presentations become nothing more than one slide of figures after another, with the finance director only providing a narrative and continuity.

At Kingstree we suggest that the challenge for the finance director is to put his or her interpretation on the numbers. The way to do that is to make a statement or 'set the scene', to create anticipation which can then be satisfied with a visual aid portraying the information graphically.

In many financial presentations the audience really has to have

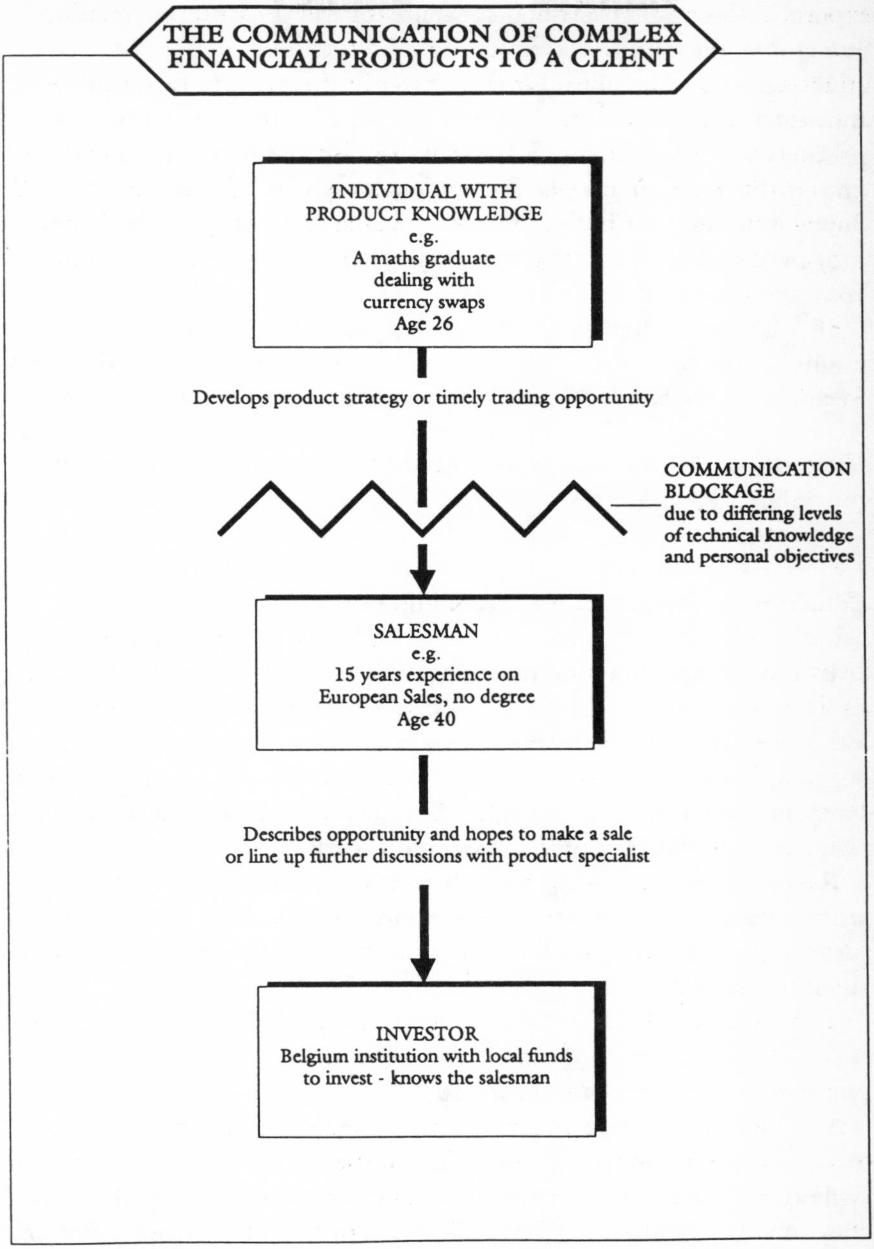

THE COMMUNICATION OF COMPLEX FINANCIAL PRODUCTS TO A CLIENT

INDIVIDUAL WITH
PRODUCT KNOWLEDGE
e.g.
A maths graduate
dealing with
currency swaps
Age 26

Develops product strategy or timely trading opportunity

COMMUNICATION
BLOCKAGE
due to differing levels
of technical knowledge
and personal objectives

SALESMAN
e.g.
15 years experience on
European Sales, no degree
Age 40

Describes opportunity and hopes to make a sale
or line up further discussions with product specialist

INVESTOR
Belgium institution with local funds
to invest - knows the salesman

Figure 4

certain figures which are too complex for the presenter to remember and quote out loud.

In these cases it is best for the figures and graphs to be given out at the end in written form. Figures should never be allowed to distract people's attention during a presentation. If the audience consists of financially minded people they might even start jotting the figures down or doing sums in their heads whilst you are talking, which means they might well miss much of what you are saying, maybe even one of your key points.

If you were to display a balance sheet, one member of the audience might focus on 'cash', another on 'fixed assets' and a third on 'receivables', while you are talking about an improvement on the liabilities side. Again, this potential for distraction can be reduced by telling the audience what they should be looking for before displaying the balance sheet itself.

Communication within the financial community

It is also critical that members of the financial community are able to communicate effectively to one another within their own organizations. Whether it is at a morning meeting where they just speak for 90 seconds suggesting an opportunity for the traders or salespeople, or at a board meeting where they have to give a full presentation, good communication skills will oil the wheels of people's work and careers.

Relying on pages of figures and thorough analysis to make a point will once again slow the pace of communication, and in some cases stop ideas getting through at all to people who can't take the time to digest the full report.

If they are reading – don't interrupt

When talking to analysts, however, it is sometimes expected that you will provide hand-outs with all figures laid out at the beginning, so that they can immediately telephone their companies with the information.

This is one of the few exceptions to the rule of not giving an audience anything that will distract them from what is being said by the speakers. It does not help the spoken communications, but it is the only way that the analysts can find the pieces of information that are relevant to them quickly.

If the audience is immersed in reading material such as this, there is no point in the speaker trying to put across any important messages at the same time. It would be better to wait for them to finish, or perhaps to take questions as they arise. If the silence is too difficult, then the speaker should just make some general, reassuring statements to set the scene.

Our advice to financial directors presenting to analysts is to be as short and succinct as possible, and then to take questions. The aim should generally be to provoke questions so that the answers can demonstrate the speaker's depth of knowledge of the areas for which he or she is responsible. They need to be aware of possible delicate areas before they start, and to be confident in their minds that they know the answers to any likely questions.

Speakers need to have the courage not to talk about too many different issues, or to go into too much detail.

If you can convince analysts that you are trustworthy and know what you are talking about, then they will accept what you say and will not expect you to justify every claim with complex calculations.

If you do go into the figures in too much depth they will firstly become bored and irritated, and then they might even begin to wonder why you are working so hard to convince them of something they were already prepared to accept.

Illustrating abstract concepts

One of the things which is happening in the financial markets today is that there are a number of products and services which have been developed, and approaches to financial engineering which are based on rather sophisticated mathematical strategies.

For example, there is the whole category of transactions which are known as 'swaps'. They are typically currency swaps or interest-rate swaps.

In order to understand these strategies one has to be dealing with them every day. Because they are arcane and frequently described by use of abstractions, they are hard for the layman to understand.

One of my colleagues, who has an MBA from Harvard, and I were preparing a young merchant banker for a presentation to his own salesforce. He was talking about a strategy which he had developed in the swaps market. The objective was to persuade the sales people to pick up their 'phones and sell the strategy to their clients around the world, providing business for the bank.

We began videotaping him on a Thursday evening and within a few minutes neither my colleague nor I could follow what he was saying.

We stopped him and explained that the audience for the presentation were going to have a similar level of financial knowledge to us. The experienced salesmen would understand the financial markets, but they could not possibly make sense of this explanation. He was going to have to simplify the story and illustrate it with concrete examples.

He went home and worked on it over the weekend and we returned on Monday evening to tape him again. This time he opened with an example of a small, relatively unknown Norwegian drilling company that needed to raise finance in Norwegian Krone, and an English pension fund which had sterling to invest.

He was able to explain a strategy that would allow his bank to put those two counter-parties together for the benefit of both, and make a profit for the bank at the same time.

This made it easy to understand, and made the sales people excited about the product.

Sample speech

The following speech was given at a European Financial Services Industry Technology Conference. It is on customer databases. The whole subject is potentially complex and dull, and the benefits could easily be too abstract for many people in the audience to grasp easily. The subject needed to be made more human.

> *Good morning, ladies and gentlemen. What's a database? Well, here's mine* (He holds up his pocket diary). *No, it's not a Filofax . . . it's my pocket diary.*
>   *It's – easy to access,*
>   *– concise,*

– well laid-out
and that simple diary
– tells me what I need to know.

That's what my database does. It's a store of information. My personal database is on paper . . . but it could just as well be on disc, or anything else.

God gave Moses his database on tablets of stone. But I wouldn't recommend that approach in this day and age!

But it's as simple and uncomplicated as that. 'Can't be', you say. And you'd be right. In the case of my diary . . . you need separate descriptions for what it is and what it does.

In the case of a commercial organization it is in fact even simpler . . . because you need one definition for both. And here's mine:

A database is an information system that makes money.

Nothing more – and never anything less.

Once you understand that . . . then you've already won half the battle. Because it is a battle. We are surrounded by information. It assails us from all sides. Only those people who know why they want the information can then set about deciding what to store and how to keep it.

The cardinal rule is: Don't store data for data's sake; Acquire it . . . Process it . . . Store it.

With one objective in mind: using your data quickly and efficiently – to make a profit!

Next to people . . . information is the prime resource of any organization. So don't abuse it, or it will abuse you. That means your data has got to be relevant as well as accurate. How often have you ploughed through a thick report brimming with facts and statistics that are all 100 per cent accurate and 0 per cent relevant? . . . Well, don't worry: that's just an example of your database costing you time and money!

So, every time you get a computerized report think 'Who's doing the work here? Me, or the data processor?'

Great, I hear you all saying . . . 'where can I buy one of these money machines?'

Well, of course, strictly speaking you can't. Spending the money isn't the problem – it's getting what you pay for that's tricky. And that requires a great deal of forethought and planning.

What I'd like to do this morning is to outline to you a process which my company is going through. I hope it'll show how we are trying to create an information system that makes money.

Our strategy involves regarding databases as just one integral part of our overall technology environment.

The investment that organizations like mine have made to create their technology environment is substantial.

And here we come to a vital lesson everybody has to learn:

– that technology has to be viewed as an investment in the business . . . not just an add-on cost.

To see what I mean, try regarding the people in your company as just another unavoidable expense . . . and see what sort of workforce you end up with.

Technology is the same. It's come a long way from the days when data processing was just a way to keep down transaction unit costs.

Oral presentations from management consultants

Another area which fascinates us is the way that major management consultancies communicate with both their existing clients and with prospects.

When a consultancy is hired to perform a particular job or project on behalf of a client, it normally conducts a study. This happens either once it's been awarded the contract, or in the course of pitching for it.

The study looks at what is going on currently in the client company, and the consultants then present their findings to various levels of management within the company or to the board itself.

Some presentations are written, but an increasing number are now oral as well.

Oral presentations become even more common once the consultants are ready to make their recommendations about what should be done to solve the problems they have been brought in to deal with.

We have found that there is a high level of skill in the consultancy industry when it comes to structuring written submissions. They nearly always provide clear, concise executive summaries at the beginning of their documents and of each section of the documents that they present, so that anyone reading them can immediately recognize the key points and follow on to explore whatever amount of detail is needed.

But when it comes to the spoken presentations, consultants rarely put into practice any of the principles which are crucial to putting across their key points.

Almost all management consultancy presentations that we have been exposed to have been slide or overhead-projector driven. They are frequently led by visual aids with lists of verbal information, frustrating the attempts of the audience to stay with the messages.

The Emperor's new clothes

One of the reasons why companies call in a consultancy like ourselves, and indeed any good management consultancy in any other area of expertise, is to benefit from our candour and objectivity.

They should not hire people like us to be yes-men and tell them what they want to hear (although a proportion do). They should rather bring us in to ask the difficult questions, where we will also be prepared to be critical or complimentary as appropriate.

It may be, for instance, that the chairman of a company is a very poor public speaker, but insists on being at the forefront as the company spokesperson at every event and new business pitch.

It is sometimes inappropriate – or even impossible – for anyone working in a company to recommend to the chairman that he should either improve his speaking techniques, or stay in the background. It may well be that the company decides to call us in to do it.

It is sometimes difficult, however, for an outsider to gauge the extent of office politics involved, particularly if he or she is new to a country, and when I first came to London I was unused to the British way of doing things.

Early on in my career in London, I was called in by the chairman of a major London bank, one of the most important people in the international financial world at the time.

During one of our sessions I asked him as a matter of routine what presentations he had coming up that we might be able to help with, at the same time as he was moving through a Kingstree training scheme.

He told me that he was due to speak to the London branch of the Harvard Business School Association on the topic of disintermediation. One of the bank's economists had prepared a draft of the speech, but I felt it was far too complex for his audience and I told him so.

I suggested that he should use it as a research piece, and pull out a few interesting key points about how banks used to work as intermediaries, and how the development of the securities industry has changed their position – hence the term 'disintermediation' – with the banks being taken out of the middle of many transactions. These should be explained in terms the audience could readily understand, and he agreed with me. But later I learnt that he had not had time to revise the speech and had delivered the original draft.

Friends of mine who were at the dinner confirmed my fears. The chairman had started by using the economist's draft, realized half way through that he had lost everyone's attention, tried to change direction and ad lib, and ended up with a presentation which was well below the standard at which he was capable of performing.

When I saw the chairman for his next session, I told him that he had missed a prime opportunity to put some key messages over to an important audience, and to sell himself and the bank. He was responsive to my suggestions and we continued the session.

After the session finished I was immediately called in to see the chief executive of the bank who was obviously very upset, and told me that it was outrageous that I should address his chairman in that way.

I told him that if I had upset the chairman by the use of inappropriate language – as a result of the cultural gap between the US and the UK – I would of course apologize to him immediately.

But if on the other hand the chief executive was suggesting that I should not have pointed out to the chairman that he had wasted a wonderful opportunity, I would not offer an apology. This was a message the chairman would not receive from anybody else in the bank and it was one he needed to hear.

The chief executive said that he supposed it was just a question of style, and I went straight to the chairman's office to apologize. The chairman then gave me some avuncular advice on the difference in business styles in Britain compared to the US – advice which I have put into practice ever since.

KEY POINTS

- The financial industry wants to hear clear visions from corporate directors
- Details should be limited in spoken financial presentations
- Figures and statistics need interpretation through metaphor, anecdote and illustration
- Statistics should rarely be key points in themselves
- Use consultants for their candour and objectivity

· 20 ·

Talking Convincingly to the Media

At Kingstree we are very much pioneers of media training, having been doing it since the early sixties. Since then, however, there have been many good books written on the subject by other practitioners, and we would agree with most of the traditional wisdom in this area. They nearly all agree with the Kingstree Approach of being yourself at all times, and of ensuring that you state your key points clearly and memorably.

When clients need media training, we approach the subject by making sure that they are aware of the requirements of the media. We do that by using a number of experienced on-camera television and radio journalists to grill our clients, after doing their homework on the industry and issues at hand.

While the journalists work on camera with the clients, the Kingstree consultants provide advice in conjunction with the public relations and communications people from the client's company.

That way we avoid the potential conflict of interests which exists if journalists who are actually working in the media are advising people whom they might, one day, have to interview.

As the media revolution continues, with more newspapers and magazines and more television and radio outlets appearing all the time, more people who are not professional broadcasters or experienced interviewees are being asked to explain their actions or to comment on events in front of cameras.

Few can resist the temptation to talk to the cameras, but it can be a daunting experience for the novice. And if the questions are in any way hostile, a professional interviewer can tie knots in anyone who isn't confident what to say and how to say it.

The media in general, and television in particular, offer people unrivalled opportunities to put their messages across to wide audiences – but it is very easy to waste those opportunities or even to do more damage than good.

Being directly questioned about anything, even in a friendly fashion, is slightly unnatural. A professional interviewer does not have time to go through all the polite rituals of getting to know you, as someone would in a social situation before starting to ask you personal or difficult questions. He or she will wade straight in.

The result is that most inexperienced interviewees become nervous and act out of character. This produces all the same disastrous results as when they act out of character in a 'live' presentation, but the cameras are taking their insincerity and spreading it out before a massive potential audience, with all the harm that that can do – not to mention the missed opportunities which positive media exposure can provide for an organization.

It is too much to expect that anyone can actually behave in a totally natural, casual manner in front of the cameras. What is possible, however, with the right training, is to 'appear' to be speaking in a normal, relaxed, conversational style.

Putting on a performance, not an act

Handling a radio or television interview is not a question of putting on an 'act', which assumes that you take on a personality which is not yours. It is more a question of giving a 'performance'.

By that I mean using your personality and knowledge to communicate the messages you need to put across to the greatest possible effect. This means heightening and dramatizing your real personality, without indulging in falsehoods.

Preparation

The illusion that many people have when going into an interview situation is that because they know more about the subject than the interviewer, which will always be the case because that is why they have been invited to appear, they will be able to 'busk it' and talk without preparation.

This is the gravest mistake they could make in most cases. To give the best possible performance it is not possible to be thinking up what you are going to say at the same time as talking.

It is critical to work out what your messages are and how you are going to get them across before you go into the studio or in front of the cameras. That way your mind will be free from stress and the influence of adrenalin while you work out the best ways of delivering the messages.

That probably means sitting down for at least a few minutes and preferably longer, jotting down the points which you want to make, and keeping them in mind throughout the interview.

If you are appearing on television you will not be able to work from notes in order to keep yourself on track, although you can if you are talking on radio or to a print journalist. For a TV interview you need to be clear in your mind what the key points are that you want to cover, so that you can tick them off in your head as you go through them.

In order to stay on track you will need to keep it simple.

Use illustrations and examples

Television is not a good medium for abstract ideas unless they are backed up by illustrations and examples. If you talk in generalities, it won't matter how many of the relevant points you have covered, the audience won't remember them.

Television audiences always have distractions, including whatever might be taking place in their own homes while they are watching. They are never listening to you in ideal situations; you therefore have to work harder to catch their attention and ensure that they hear what you want them to hear, and that your messages are memorable.

Knowing too much

The more you know about your subject the more crucial it is that you prepare yourself in advance, because of the time limitations.

The average interview time on radio or television is two and a half minutes, which gives you very little time to put across a lifetime's experience of a subject.

If you have broad knowledge of a subject you may be tempted to go into too much detail, which will result in a loss of the audience's attention and a failure to get as far as delivering the key messages.

Many inexperienced interviewees make the mistake of approaching an interview like an educational examination: expecting to be asked questions which will test their knowledge of their subject.

This couldn't be further from the truth. The interviewers are going to assume that you have a knowledge of your subject, otherwise you wouldn't be there. They merely want to get the most relevant pieces of information out of you on behalf of their audiences.

The more knowledgeable and intelligent the prospective interviewees are, the more likely they are to believe that they can talk off the tops of their heads, and the less likely they are to be able to do that in reality.

It is easy to underestimate the power of television cameras and lights, and of the technicians who treat you as if you are just one more widget on an assembly line, to make someone who is normally confident and eloquent into a sweating, stuttering mess.

Someone who is unfamiliar with the medium and who doesn't prepare will always regret it.

Simple messages are best

Often the greatest orators say the least complex things.

Many of the politicians, showbusiness personalities and union leaders who are most frequently quoted in the media are the ones with the least to say. What they do have to say, however, is very clear and concise and frequently repeated.

They know how to speak in language which listeners, viewers and readers can easily catch and remember.

You therefore need to work out in advance what those most interesting points are and, if possible turn them into Sound Bites.

Create Sound Bites

Sound Bites are succinct phrases or sentences which sum up your arguments and make them memorable.

'The Lady's not for turning' from Mrs Thatcher, for instance, or 'Read my Lips' from President Bush, or 'He would say that, wouldn't he' from Mandy Rice Davies.

The media love these sorts of quotes because they provide them with headlines, and because their audiences like them. It doesn't matter if they are clichés, as long as they convey the right messages.

Everyone has a number of demands on his or her time and memories. You cannot expect any audience to remember large amounts of what you have to say. What they can remember is catch-phrases.

If you get your Sound Bites right they could even end up as famous quotations. In fact many of the world's most influential speech-writers start by inventing Sound Bites for their clients, and then build speeches around them.

You could do the same when you are preparing your notes. What you need are telling phrases which will act as memory triggers to the audience long after your image has left the screen.

Impressions and credibility

Interviews are largely a question of credibility and impressions. If you don't come across as a credible spokesperson for your cause, it won't matter what you have to say because people will not believe you or want to listen to you.

If you are the chief executive of an airline attending the scene of a crash, people watching have to believe (a) that you are truly compassionate and caring about the distress of the victims and their families, and (b) that you are actually able and willing to do something about finding out what went wrong and ensuring that it doesn't happen again – as far as that is possible.

The information which you are imparting may or may not remain with the audience after your image has faded from the screen, but the impression which you have made will linger on in their minds, for good or bad.

Unless, of course, you make no impression at all – in which case there is little point in being there.

The positive attitude

Too many interviewees simply react to the questions which the interviewers put to them, either because they are overawed by the experience of being in a television studio, or because they believe that that is what is expected of them.

In fact it is the exact opposite. The interviewers like nothing better than someone who is pro-active, full of life and talk and ideas, and who gives the audience good value for money.

If you are there to talk on a particularly contentious subject and you seem to be evading the issues, then they may try to pursue you with questions. In most cases, however, they will be quite happy to let you steer the way the conversation goes, provided you are being interesting and/or entertaining.

If there has been a major disaster, like an aircrash or an oil spillage, or a financial fraud, the chances are that the interviewee is spending most of his or her waking hours dealing with the resulting problems.

He will therefore be used to appearing to take responsibility for what has happened, and may well look as if he is carrying the weight of the world on his shoulders.

If he is then asked to speak to the cameras, it is vital not to carry this attitude with him. If you look and sound as if you have all the woes of the world on your shoulders you will give audiences all the wrong signals.

If they weren't alarmed before, they will be by your appearance. If they didn't think it was your fault before, they will assume they were wrong because that is the impression you are giving.

Putting things into perspective

The trick is to put things into perspective.

If, for instance, you are a spokesperson for a railway system and you are called in front of the cameras to answer questions on why so many trains are delayed or cancelled, it is all too easy to look guilty and to start making excuses.

In reality your railway system may carry millions of people to work and back every day, only a tiny proportion of whom suffer delays and inconvenience.

By pointing out these facts, and putting the problem into perspective, you demonstrate that you are in control of the situation and knowledgeable about the subject. You can then go on to show that you appreciate the problems of those who are delayed, and convince the audience that you will do your best to alleviate them wherever possible.

An audience will always be sympathetic to reasoned arguments if they like and trust the person who is speaking.

Take control

The natural instinct for most interviewees, therefore, is to wait to be asked a question, give an answer and then stop talking, waiting for the next question. This is the wrong approach.

If you allow an interviewer to control the conversation you could end up wasting valuable time talking about things which are of no relevance to your key messages.

You should be determined to get your key points across, almost irrespective of the questions which the interviewer is asking.

If an interviewer is pursuing a line of questioning which does not seem to you to be going anywhere, there is no reason why you should follow, and thereby waste the opportunity for putting across something positive and useful.

There are many polite and reasonable conversational devices for changing the track of the interview:

'Yes but surely the most important point to remember is . . .'

'That's true, but at the same time, don't forget that . . .'

With these simple devices, which you wouldn't hesitate to use in normal conversation, you can steer the interviewer back to your main points.

There is no reason to give the interviewer control of the conversation. It is much better to take control yourself. Tell him what he should be asking and why, explain the good things that you and your company are doing, and put things into perspective.

Whenever possible encapsulate your argument in your first sentence, and then spend the rest of the interview backing it up, preferably with good colourful or concrete examples.

This is particularly true when you are dealing with bad news.

If taken too far, of course, this could make you appear either evasive or bullying, but if the normal courtesies of casual conversation are observed, it will create the impression that you are sure of your opinions and eloquent in expressing them.

When Margaret Thatcher resigned, a programme was made about the interviews which she had given during her tenure.

Sir Robin Day, the distinguished interviewer, was asked if there was any question which he would like to have asked the Prime Minister but had never dared to.

Sir Robin said yes, he would like to have opened an interview with the words, 'Prime Minister, what is your answer to my first question?'

Obviously, if you consistently refuse to answer questions and do not treat your interviewers with the courtesy which they might expect in a normal conversation, you will give the wrong impression and alienate your audience.

You must always give your audience the impression that you are having a normal conversation with your interviewer, but you must remain determined at all times to get your points across.

The commercial element

The value of a television interview in commercial terms is enormous. If you work out the cost of buying two minutes of television airtime for a commercial, and then add the cost of actually making the film, you begin to see the potential of an interview.

Let's say, for the sake of argument, that it would cost a quarter of a million pounds to buy that amount of time and fill it with a high quality commercial during peak viewing time.

Would it not be madness to waste the opportunity to get all that for free? Would it not be almost criminal to wander into the studio with no idea what your key messages are or how you are going to put them across?

There should always be a commercial element in any interview given by a business person, otherwise there is no reason to do it.

In most cases that will mean you are either performing a damage limitation exercise or you are working to increase public awareness of whatever it is you are doing. If it is the former you will be explaining why something has gone wrong, putting it into perspective and giving listeners confidence that you are dealing with the situation and preventing it occurring again; in the latter case you will be attempting to make what your company is doing interesting.

Non-verbal signals

Because television is such a visual medium, the non-verbal signals which you give acquire an even greater significance than they might in live speaking situations.

The way you sit or stand could easily give the lie to the words you are saying.

If you are trying to put across a strong, positive message, and your body appears tense and ill at ease, the audience will receive conflicting messages, and will either disbelieve or discount whatever you are saying.

A survey testing the impact of television interviews on their audiences came up with some surprising results.

It discovered that a mere six per cent of the impact was attributed to the actual words being spoken; 37 per cent was attributed to the way the words were used, the tone of voice and the relationship between the interviewer and interviewee, and 57 per cent to the way the person dressed, moved, stood and presented him or herself.

In other words the major impact came from the impression made on the eye, not the ear.

Dress

What is required when appearing in the media is 'appropriate dress'. This means clothes which reinforce the messages being put across.

Viewers expect certain modes of dress from certain types of people, and to surprise them means distracting them from what you are saying.

If you have just emerged from a coalmine it would be ridiculous to be dressed in a pin-stripe suit, and if you are the chairman of a major company it would be inappropriate to be seen in grimy overalls when commenting on the financial performance of the company, (it might, however, be highly appropriate if you are demonstrating how the company's senior management is willing to get its hands dirty on the shop floor).

If you are a senior economist but you dress like a social worker you will be sending out contradictory messages to your audiences, and that is an unnecessary complication.

Remember: THE EYE ALWAYS TAKES PRECEDENCE OVER THE EAR. IF AN AUDIENCE SEES ONE THING AND HEARS ANOTHER IT WILL BE THE THINGS WHICH THEY SEE THAT THEY WILL REMEMBER.

Sitting and standing

The aim with any posture is to appear authoritative, and to give the impression that you are likely to answer questions honestly and competently.

If you perform distracting movements with your hands the audience may spend their time discussing what you are doing rather than listening to what you are saying.

That could mean shifting from foot to foot, or tugging on your ear lobe or the end of your nose. Whatever it is it will be accentuated by the camera and will distract attention.

If you are sitting, it is a mistake to think that lounging will give the impression that you are relaxed: it will give the impression that you are not interested in what you are saying, which will have the effect of making the audience equally uninterested.

The best sitting position is upright, leaning slightly forward.

If you are sitting in a swivel chair, do not sway back and forth – it is distracting and looks shifty and nervous, as if you are searching for an avenue of escape.

If you are standing, the least distracting position is with your feet about eight inches apart and your weight evenly distributed between them.

If you normally use your hands when you talk, then do the same on screen, but if you normally keep them still don't try to change or you will appear self-conscious.

If you do not know what to do with your hands then it is best to keep them in front of you, with one hand clasping the wrist of the other.

Men should try to avoid having both hands cupped over the crotch in a position which professionals refer to as 'the executive fig leaf.'

Avoid putting your hands in your pockets – particularly if you might jingle your change nervously.

Avoid distracting backgrounds

Television programme makers tend to encourage interviewees to stand in front of busy backgrounds, since that gives a more interesting picture.

For the speaker it is counter-productive and the plainer the background the more likely it is the viewer is to listen to what is being said. Anything which is seen should reinforce the image which the speaker wants to put across.

The role of the press officer

In companies of any size it is always a good idea to have a central press office through which enquiries can be channelled, and which anyone asked to do an interview can use for advice.

It gives people someone to bounce ideas off and someone who will know what approaches the producers and interviewers on various programmes are likely to take.

Every interview carries some risks, and it is always better to be prepared for what those risks are likely to be. A press officer will be particularly helpful if you are likely to be subjected to any sort of investigative or aggressive questioning.

NEVER SAY 'NO COMMENT' – because it looks like an admission of guilt.

Sometimes the media will take you completely by surprise, asking you to comment on something which you didn't even know had happened, at a time when you did not expect to have to talk to anyone.

When that happens you need to be prepared to co-operate as much as you can, and to admit to being taken by surprise. e.g.

'This is the first I have heard of this tragedy, and obviously if it is true we will act immediately to find out the facts and put it right. I will talk to my managing director and come back to you with all the information as soon as I can.'

You must immediately appear competent, in control and caring. It will be hard to do that if you have not prepared yourself in advance for the possibility of an event of this sort.

Remain calm

No matter how much pressure you are put under, never become angry with the media. You will never win an argument like this because the other people hold all the cards.

They have nothing to lose – in fact if you lose your temper they may even have a better programme. You, however, have a great deal to lose – and a great deal to gain by handling it right.

Jargon

A television audience is the least able to tolerate jargon, since it is so widely based. The sort of 'corporate-speak' which is quite normal in the business world sounds pretentious and absurd when used in the media.

Whatever the subject you should always use chatty, colloquial language, with some concessions to the particular programme, (e.g. if on the *Money Programme* you should take a different tone from that you would use on *Wogan*).

The image to bear in mind at all times is that you are talking to an acquaintance who has an interest in, but no special technical knowledge of, what you are saying.

In some cases the more esoteric the jargon is, the less harmful. If you are talking about a particularly complex scientific subject, the audience will expect not to understand all the words you use – although they must still understand the messages.

The worst sort of jargon is the use of every-day words in specialized ways – something which the legal profession has been doing for centuries, which is why it is so widely distrusted by the general public.

Management and computing experts are equally guilty of making simple messages complex with distorted use of language.

Treat the interview like a conversation

This cannot be stated too often or too firmly. If you are in any doubt about how to handle some aspect of an interview, keep telling yourself that you are simply having a conversation with the interviewer, and that the camera is merely there to observe.

That means that you look at the interviewer as often as you would in a normal conversation, and that you never look directly at the camera.

This convention is particularly strong in the UK, although in America it is sometimes permissible to look into the camera and talk directly to the audience.

The exception to this rule is if you are talking 'down the line' to the interviewer. This means talking on the telephone, with your face appearing on a screen beside the interviewer. In those cases you are usually sitting in a studio on your own, staring into the camera lens, trying to imagine that you are looking into the eyes of the interviewer.

This takes place more and more as the technology of television becomes more sophisticated. It also happens in radio interviews, where the interviewee is sometimes even given a key to a cell-like room and expected to operate the microphone, with no human contact apart from voices in a pair of headphones.

How we deal with clients

When clients first come to us for media coaching, we start by sitting them in front of the camera and asking them general questions, such as what their companies do and what their jobs involve.

These are questions to which they must know the answers, and that is where they go wrong because they invariably start to waffle.

We can then show them the results and they are able to see immediately how important it is to be prepared.

Because they have given no thought to what they are going to say, what audience they are addressing, how long they are going to be talking for, or what their key messages should be – because we have given them no warning – they usually look and sound terrible, and are never able to give the best account possible of themselves, which is what we trust that all our clients will be able to achieve on all occasions, after our training.

This acts as a warning of just what is going to happen if they do not do their groundwork. If they can't talk effectively about their jobs and their companies in a relatively informal atmosphere, how can they cope with any difficult questions which might come along in a more formal one?

The idea is the same as aversion therapy. We want to make them feel uncomfortable, so that they will not take the risk of the same thing happening in a real situation.

We then discuss why it is that they have found such a simple exercise so difficult – for all the reasons which we have discussed in this chapter – and get them to think about the main points which they want to put across.

We then help them to work on all the aspects where they have come across badly, and to identify what their key messages are going to be.

We advise them that once they have stated their key points they should not issue any new information, since it will only serve to make the viewer forget the preceding messages.

Questions to ask yourself before an interview

● *Why should I do this interview?*

- *Whom am I addressing?*
- *How long have I got to speak?*
- *What messages do I want the audience to remember or what do I want them to do after the programme?*

Once you know the answers to these questions you can start to think about your key points and your Sound Bites.

Questions to ask other people

While preparing yourself, between the moment when you decide to do the interview and actually doing it, you need to try to find out a few things from the programme makers:

- *How is the item going to be introduced?* (That is, what will the viewer have seen or heard before you come on?)
- *Is anyone else going to be interviewed on the same subject?* (I mean interviewed individually: I am not dealing with group discussions here.)
- *What angle are they likely to take?* (Their name and that of their organization will probably be enough to indicate that.)
- *Who is your interviewer going to be?* (It probably won't be the same person as the researcher or scriptwriter who chats to you on the phone.)
- *Is the interview going to be done live, or recorded?* (If live, how long will it run? If recorded, how long will you be interviewed for, and, most important, how long will the broadcast version be? If there is more than a minute's difference between the two, you must be extra careful to stick to your key points. This is the most effective safeguard you have against the possibility that the edited version will carry a different emphasis from the one you intended.)
- *What is the interviewer going to ask you about?*
- *What will the first question be?*

The interviewer will tell you the topics he wants to cover in his questions but not the specific phrasing of any question other than the first, nor indeed in which order he will deal with the topics. He wants to avoid the interview appearing stilted, and will prefer it to develop naturally, his second question depending on how you answer the first one.

If during discussion with him you feel he is not going to give you the opportunity to introduce one of your key points, tell him why you think it is so pertinent and interesting. If he is convinced (and you are the expert, so most likely he will be) he will frame a suitable question.

You won't always be able to get full answers to all these questions, and this is where a press officer can be helpful for background on the programme makers.

Most interviews are not confrontational. In the majority of cases the interviewers share with the interviewees a wish to leave the viewer better informed. That should lead to collaboration rather than confrontation.

It is also important to be aware when the interview is about to end. The signal is often given by the interviewer, who will make a winding up sign (previously agreed with you) when there are 15 seconds to go, giving the interviewees a chance to wind up what they are saying and leave the viewers with some clear messages.

The basic approach should be the same for TV, radio and press interviews in terms of doing the essential preparation and putting the issues into perspective.

A crucial difference with press interviews is that they are open-ended, and it is advisable to set a time-limit at the beginning, to avoid wasting time.

In telephone interviews never speak off the cuff; always offer to ring back after you have given the matter some thought. This will also allow you to check that the interviewer is indeed who he or she claims to be.

It is harder to put across your personality in radio interviews. There is less sense of occasion than in a TV studio so you need to psych yourself up to performance level. Do not be stampeded into talking without time for preparation.

It is nearly always worth accepting invitations to radio 'phone-ins and television panel discussions – but always prepare your key points in advance. On a panel you need to be aggressive to catch the chairman's eye, and you should deliver your key points quickly in case you are not given another chance. Whenever someone else makes a point, register your feelings with a nod or shake of the head – or something more dramatic. Directors of this type of programme are always looking for something interesting to show. If you are lively when others are dead-pan, you will get the lion's share of camera time. It is important, of course, not to over-act.

How to present and perform for the video camera

Performing on video is becoming a more commonplace management task every year, yet many people find it just as terrifying as, if not more so, than standing up on a stage or being interviewed for broadcast television.

At least in front of an audience you get feedback, but when you are being stared at by the cold eye of the camera you get nothing, and you can be left feeling very lonely and rather foolish.

Most people in management have become accustomed to the presence of a video camera in training sessions of one sort or another. They might, for instance, have used it for role playing when developing interviewing skills, or any other inter-personal skills training.

At Kingstree we use the cameras extensively, as they provide the only practical way in which our clients can be shown how they come across to others, and what radical improvements can be made with relatively minor adjustments.

In this sort of situation it does not take long to get used to the camera being there, since it is really just acting like a fly on the wall and you can continue to behave as you would if it were not there.

In some exercises we make a point of video-taping clients who are unaware that the camera is switched on.

We do this to show them a stark contrast between their own innate, relaxed communication style and the way they begin to perform when we put them through more formal exercises, which we also record.

We can then compare the two ways that the client talks by playing the tapes side by side. That establishes in the client's mind his or her own model of excellence for how to behave when under stress.

If you are asked to make a corporate video, or a presentation over the video conferencing lines, or to perform on a company television show, the pressures are going to be very different. Suddenly you are confronted with the debilitating effects of traditional stage-fright, mixed with techno-fear since most people have no idea what all the equipment around them is actually for. Some people thrive on this stress, many more find it uncomfortable.

To begin with you will be in the hands of your director or producer. He or she will tell you whether to talk directly to the camera (unlikely unless you are very experienced), or to someone else in the studio, or to an interviewer who is sitting just off camera.

Once you know the guidelines, however, you need to employ all your own spoken communication skills in the same way as you would if making a presentation to a live audience.

You need to prepare notes beforehand, which you might in some cases be able to refer to. You should pause to let your thoughts sink in, and you should aim to make your performance as close to the style you adopt in casual conversation as is possible under such artificial conditions.

The trap which many people fall into is to see the cameras and start 'acting' whatever part they think they have been cast in, whether it is chairman of the board or technical expert from the laboratories.

The camera can spot insincere, unnatural behaviour just as quickly as the human eye, and the audiences will immediately lose interest in watching the results. Also, this switch into a role is usually accompanied by a lapse into jargon and stilted language, which makes it hard for the television viewers to take in the key points.

Unless the audiences are watching under controlled circumstances, such as in a training session or at a conference, they will always have the option of turning off or walking away from the set, thereby robbing you of your opportunity to communicate your messages.

Video-conferencing

Video-conferencing is another growth area of spoken communication. While I personally believe that it will never replace the face-to-face meeting as the most effective way of doing business, there certainly is a place for it when international meetings are required which do not merit the time and expense of travel, or when there is an urgent need for a visual exchange of information.

It is a medium which fits into the business communications mix somewhere between live meetings and telephone conversations.

For the participants in a video-conference, there can still be a level of nervousness caused by the presence of the camera and other technology, although most people relax quickly and begin to talk in a fairly normal manner once the meeting gets under way.

Because it is an expensive medium, it requires users to be disciplined in their approach, unlike the live meeting which can stretch out at either end and is interrupted by telephone calls or people leaving the room for whatever reason.

Anyone using video-conferencing facilities, therefore, needs to plan the presentation as for a formal live meeting – say to the board of directors: to open with key points and have one core theme. Interaction from the other end of the conversation can then develop the theme.

There are usually monitors showing the broadcasters how they are looking to the other end, and if possible these should be ignored, except when checking that the right people are on screen or the correct flip chart or document is being sent down the line.

By concentrating on the faces of the people at the other end of the broadcast, just as on news programmes or chat shows where reporters and guests appear via satellite screen, it is relatively easy to simulate casual conversation until it comes naturally.

In-house video and video conferencing facilities are communication tools which people in business will find they are being asked to use more and more in the future. Just as with the telephone, there are right and wrong ways to use them, but there is no reason to fear them, provided you train and prepare correctly.

KEY POINTS

- Be prepared for the effects of stress
- List key messages – as few as possible
- Put on a performance – not an act
- Keep the messages simple
- Interviewers and journalists primarily want information for their audiences
- Create Sound Bites
- Have a positive attitude
- Take control of interviews
- The eye takes precedence over the ear
- Use press officers constructively
- Cut out all jargon
- Interviews are just conversations with a much larger audience
- Television conveys impressions not details
- Use illustrations and examples
- Be aware of non-verbal signals
- Remain calm at all times
- Use in-house video and video-conferencing as presentation aids

· 21 ·

Handling Question and Answer Sessions

The question and answer sessions at the end of a presentation are an opportunity for members of the audience to pursue their own special interests and concerns.

They are also opportunities for the presenters to demonstrate the depth and breadth of their knowledge and to give a further insight into their personalities. Handled the wrong way they can give completely the opposite to the desired impression.

Always pause

After a question is asked, presenters should always pause before answering.

This pause is significant in three ways:

First it restrains the presenter from making a hasty statement that may not address the question, and allows time to formulate a succinct reply.

Second, it allows the audience to see the presenter formulating a thoughtful response.

Third, it gives value to the question, and to the questioner, by showing that thought is required before answering.

Keep it short

Concise responses are usually more effective than elaborate ones. People are often more interested in their own questions than in the answers they receive. A short answer is rarely a problem because if the audience needs more information they will ask for it with a follow-up question.

On the other hand, long answers which can sometimes qualify as 'mini-speeches' will bore the audience and cause them to switch off.

Many people, particularly those with a deep interest in and knowledge of their subjects, are tempted into allowing their answers to ramble. In some cases that can be positively dangerous, giving an aggressive questioner information which can be used out of context to hit back at you later.

I was working with the president of a major international oil company on just this problem. His public affairs department had suggested that I might like to ask him about the company's poor record for equal employment opportunity, because at the time the company had no officers from any minority groups, including women.

I duly asked him the question and he answered it superbly by explaining how everyone who joined the company had exactly the same chances of rising to the top. It was a text-book example of how to answer a potentially damaging question.

When he had finished this highly effective answer, however, I did not speak. I merely continued to look at him, and he couldn't resist the temptation to continue.

'For example,' he said, 'look at my own case, I started out from a poor family, when we were young . . .' and he proceeded to paint a picture of himself as being, in the American term, 'poor white trash'.

After listening to this long biographical diatribe I looked up from a copy of the company's report and accounts and asked him how he could possibly attempt to paint himself as 'poor white trash' with an income of however many hundreds of thousands of dollars it was, not to mention share holdings and options.

He was so shocked to be attacked for something which he had imagined showed him in a good light that he couldn't even come up with an answer.

The point was that I had taken something he had said completely out of context, and twisted it to fit my own needs. My question did not make any particularly damaging point about his company, but it made him look foolish and boastful, undermined his credibility and as a result destroyed the excellent answer which he had given at the beginning.

When we played him back the video of the session, the president was so horrified to watch the tape of him digging a hole for himself, and to see how well he would have answered if he had taken our advice and quit while he was ahead, that he asked me to fly back from California to the East Coast to re-run another question and answer session with him the following week.

Always admit to not knowing

Presenters should also remember that it is no sin to admit to not knowing something. Most listeners realize that no-one has all the answers on any subject at split-second command. This is particularly true at annual general meetings.

Always listen to the entire question before answering, and do not begin forming your answer in your mind while the question is being asked. Most people ask rambling questions, so listen to it in its entirety, then think about what your answer is.

If you sense that a questioner is beginning to ask a multi-faceted question, take notes. It is then often possible to select one specific point, or rephrase the whole question, before answering it. This will be much harder to do if you fail to jot down the key points of each question as they are being put.

If necessary, repeat the question so that everyone in the room can hear it. That will flatter the questioner and give you more time to formulate a reply. You still need to pause before answering to compose your thoughts.

Watch out for presumptive questions which are not based on fact, and point them out to the questioners rather than getting trapped into giving an answer to a question which is wrong.

Beware of loaded questions

Always beware of 'loaded' questions laced with inflammatory or prejudiced adverbs and adjectives. The chances are that these questioners have already made up their minds what the answers should be and just want you to become partisan and confirm their prejudices.

If you were an executive of the Boeing aircraft company, for instance, you might be faced with a question which started:

'Since the Boeing Company is no longer the recognized international leader in the commercial aircraft industry, how do you justify. . . ?'

The initial presumption is obviously wrong since Boeing maintains the lion's share of it's market, but if the executive fails to contradict the original assumption, other members of the audience will assume that the questioner's statement is true.

It is surprising how many people when answering loaded questions will ignore the presumption at the beginning because they are concentrating on their answer.

If a question is patently outrageous it can be better to resist answering the question at all, and simply say to the individual, 'Oh come on now, you know that is a loaded question . . .' and pass on to take the next question without dignifying the loaded one with an answer. This will usually generate a sympathetic response from other people in the room – unless you are using the technique simply as a way of evading a difficult question.

The moment you respond to a question which is clearly outrageous, you put yourself into a gutter fight with a snake, and you are unlikely to win.

When you encounter one of those questions which are in fact small speeches and not questions at all, you might ask exactly what the question is rather than trying to guess.

At new business pitches

At a competitive business pitch there is always the danger of a question which highlights an area of weakness in the pitching company.

The temptation then is to become very defensive with the answers when what is needed is a positive approach. It is always better to give a short, succinct answer in these circumstances, rather than set off on a self-justifying ramble.

Everyone has strengths and weaknesses and if there is a problem in a certain area it is better to be honest about it and say 'Yes, that is an area we want to develop, and this is what we are doing about it'.

Always give the impression that you are being fair and honest.

The secret is to be yourself at all times when answering questions, and to talk to the questioners just as if you were in a normal conversation. That means that you can use humour, silence and the questioner's name – if you know it – just as you would in a meeting or at a cocktail or dinner party.

Beware of giving out too much information. This is a particular danger if the questioner hits on a subject which really interests you, and which you have not covered in detail in the presentation. There may be a strong temptation to get onto your hobby horse. Even if you retain the interest of the questioner by doing this, you still run the risk of alienating others in the audience who have less interest in this aspect of the subject.

Just answer the question which is asked. If people want to know more they will ask for it. Do not allow one answer to trigger a whole stream of connected thoughts which lead you off at tangents.

Hecklers

In some cases, particularly annual general meetings, a speaker might come up against professional hecklers, people who have been sent in specifically to ask embarrassing questions, or who are naturally difficult.

Although in many cases questions will have been pre-submitted, the ones which have been seen before the meeting may simply be a lead in to something which the presenter is not expecting and which may be aggressive.

There is a right way to handle such people without alienating the rest of the audience. They need to be handled firmly and with humour. The speaker, however, must be careful not to be derogatory: in that way there will be a natural tendency for the audience to come onto your side.

If, for instance, someone is persistent in asking why red telephone boxes have been removed and replaced by less attractive high-tech models, he or she may demand to know what is being done about it, and claim to have written on many occasions without receiving a satisfactory response.

The person answering this question needs to be aware of why red telephone boxes were impractical – being subject to vandalism and frequently used as lavatories – and perhaps have some figures available on the increased percentage of public telephones now in working order. It should also be possible to refer to the number of red boxes which have been maintained in areas of particular scenic interest.

KEY POINTS

- Remember the pauses
- Keep it short
- Never pretend you know something you don't
- Always listen to the whole question
- Always correct erroneous assumptions
- Be positive

· 22 ·

Crisis Management

Crisis management is one of the most stressful experiences which can happen to managers. It only happens occasionally, so no-one ever grows experienced at it, but mishandling a crisis can bring a company to its knees almost overnight, so it is vital to get it right. The Bhopal chemical plant disaster in India is a good example.

It might be an oil company dealing with a spillage which is polluting a coastline, an airline dealing with a crash of one of its planes or a company confronted with evidence of fraud among its employees. Whatever it is, you need to be able to persuade listening and watching people that you are in control and you are doing your best to limit the damage and deal with the vital human issues.

Here the key is to plan ahead. All good crisis management starts with the recognition that a crisis could occur at anytime in the future.

You need to research all the possible scenarios which could evolve from the crisis. This will include determining who will be affected, what services might be interrupted, what emergency services need to be alerted, and establishing well in advance which specific individual or team will respond to the onset of a crisis.

Naturally, this is a complex subject which could readily justify a book of its own. Clearly there are operational issues to be confronted, but these fall outside the scope of these views on spoken communication. Equally, there are areas where operational and communication issues overlap.

It might be appropriate to install toll-free telephone lines which are only activated in an actual crisis, to provide information to people who are involved, and to nominate spokespeople at remote locations as well as company headquarters. A company should also determine in advance what their statements will be concerning liability, assignment of blame etc.

Different industries face widely varying potential scenarios, some of which have a number of facets common to threats in other industries, while some are unique.

Senior airline executives, for instance, talking to media at the scene of a crash cannot afford to become too emotional or too defensive. While they will obviously be shocked by what has happened, the important thing for them to do is disseminate information in a concise, objective way.

While showing sympathy for victims, they also need to show loyalty to their employees and not start apportioning blame. Listeners have to come away with a positive impression that everything that could be done is being done, and that continuing operations are being carried out correctly and efficiently.

A perfect example of this was demonstrated when a British Midland Airways plane crashed onto the M1 motorway in Britain. The company's chief executive, Michael Bishop, was immediately on the scene and dealt with the situation admirably. He was a credit to his company at a critical time. Badly handled, the disaster could have resulted in irreparable damage to British Midland, and that is how high the stakes can sometimes be when senior executives are called on to speak on behalf of their companies.

Under this sort of pressure it is even harder to deal with impertinent accusations from aggressive journalists, but they have to be dealt with, and they have to be dealt with immediately. If the executives start saying 'no comment' and then go away to prepare a carefully worded statement, which they issue the following day, the damage will already have been done. People will believe the company has something to hide and will not have had the opportunity of seeing them performing honourably under pressure.

As in so many other situations, the listeners want to see and hear people they trust and like. Their initial reaction to something like an aircrash or a leakage of industrial chemicals, is to hunt out a scapegoat. That scapegoat will be the chief executive or spokesperson of the company concerned.

If, however, when they come in to attack, they find someone reasonable and intelligent, who is not trying to shirk the responsibility, but is able to bring calm and reason to the situation, they will immediately begin to modify their potentially hostile or inflammatory opinions.

It is like watching a well-written courtroom drama; when the prosecution sums up, you feel sure that he is right and the jury must put the accused away for life. But the moment the equally skilled defence puts the other point of view you see another side, and you will then find yourself sympathetic to all the players in the drama.

This is because the scriptwriters and actors are putting real people in front of you, people with whom you can identify. That skill elicits your understanding and forbearance. Executives dealing with crises must put their cases before their audiences in just the same way, presenting their true personality strengths and integrity while operating under pressure.

Countering subjective judgements

Whenever it comes to convincing people of the rightness of a corporate action, whether it is to do with air safety or protection of the environment, in the final analysis the convincing has to be done by someone standing up and talking.

It comes down to the power of someone's personality and communication skill as to whether they will be able to calm nerves, convince people of the truth of their case, and cater for the subjectivity of all our approaches to contentious issues.

Whenever someone stands in front of an audience to deliver a message, before the spokesperson has even begun to speak, the audience will be making subjective assessments as to whether or not he or she is trustworthy, confident, intelligent or well informed. If you respect someone from that initial response you are then more likely to listen to the message.

To engender this sort of respect speakers have to be able to project their personalities, and demonstrate that they are willing to come up and speak their minds, that they are not just going to say something to cover themselves and then scuttle back into the shadows.

A speaker dealing with a crisis must show willingness to be in charge, agree that something has gone wrong and demonstrate that they will do something about it.

If there is an oil spillage at sea people want to see senior executives at the scene and hear them explaining exactly what they are doing to minimize the damage. They are then more likely to listen to the company's explanations as to what went wrong.

A company that chooses to keep a low profile, and tries to avoid speaking to anyone on the subject, is likely to engender considerable hostility from the public and no matter how big it is that sort of feeling can adversely affect its business or even hit the share price.

Individual personalities communicating directly will always win the day over anonymous corporations.

Internal communications

It isn't just the words which are spoken to the outside world through the media which are important. It is also critical that management as a whole is trained and able to communicate messages clearly and consistently throughout the company in a time of crisis.

If a company appears in the papers because of some scandal, everyone who works for that company is likely to be questioned by relatives, friends and acquaintances. Untold damage can be done if these people receive the wrong messages, because they will start unfounded rumours which will grow and spread very quickly.

The messages which are formed at the top must be communicated throughout the company, with the key points stressed at every level, so that everyone understands them, believes in them and remembers them.

KEY POINTS

- Plan for disaster
- Put things into perspective
- Be willing to admit mistakes
- Counter subjectivity
- Be willing to take charge
- Communicate the key messages to the whole company

· 23 ·

How the System Works for Politicians and Diplomats

Kingstree as a company started life by serving the needs of the political establishment, because politicians down the ages have always recognized the importance and value of effective spoken communication.

We still work with politicians and diplomats at all levels, although they have now been overtaken by the world of business in the quantity of people eager to learn the secrets of successful presentation.

In England there is a tradition of politicians, civil servants and diplomats being able to give 'background' briefings to the media which are off the record and not for attribution. In America there is no such principle. There, every public figure who stands up and says something has to assume that there is someone from the media there who might quote whatever is said – possibly out of context.

That means that no-one in a prominent position can afford to talk off top of their heads.

For any politician or diplomat, the difference between long-term success or failure will rest very largely on people's perception of their personalities. In the case of politicians they have to overcome a high degree of distrust amongst the general public who, often quite rightly, find it hard to believe in politicians' sincerity.

If, when they make speeches or talk to the media, they are stiff and unnatural, they will not inspire confidence or trust, and will not be able to persuade people to vote for them when the time comes. Nor will they be able to persuade people of the rightness of any causes which they might espouse during their careers.

By communicating effectively, and using proven tools for capturing and holding audience attention, they can increase the impact of everything they say, and will be able to avoid blundering into areas where they might be poorly-informed and in danger of saying the wrong things.

The Conservatives communicate

One of my colleagues at Kingstree is Neil Chalmers, who came to us from Saatchi & Saatchi, where he was a director and where, among other things, he had been working on the Conservative Party account.

The Conservatives are a good example of a political party which realized the importance of communications, did something about it and reaped enormous rewards as a result.

They first went to Saatchi & Saatchi in 1977. Their problem was that the forms of communication which political parties can enter into (between elections) with their various audiences are limited.

The parties are funded in such a way that they can only spend money promoting individuals at times of election. So party political broadcasts and the performance of the individual members of parliament were the only vehicles which they had for putting across their messages. The business world at the end of the 70s was short of funds and so, consequently, was the Party.

There had been a period of disarray in politics as a whole, and it was decided that the Party needed to take the high ground strategically and identify those areas which most concern the electorate if it was to emerge as the winner.

The first step, therefore, was to undertake a rigorous, on-going research programme to find out what it was that the audience (ie. the voting public), wanted to see done, so that they could decide what the key messages of their campaign should be. They also wanted to know how their various senior players in the Party rated with the public.

From that data the Central Office research department could then put together very clear briefs concerning individual areas of policy development, and develop lines of strategy which would interest the voters.

They identified inflation as the key issue which everyone was worried about at the time. So bringing it down became their main electoral platform. In 1979 Margaret Thatcher swept to power on just that ticket.

By the time of the next election in 1983 the Falklands War had taken place, and the message was that the country was now on its way to prosperity and strength, and there must be no turning back.

Research after that showed that the public rated Mrs Thatcher herself highly, rated what she had done highly, but couldn't quite identify what she was going to do next. She was re-elected, however, on the strength of what had gone before, and by the 1987 election the Party had grown used to the concept of thinking strategically. It now planned what it was going to do well in advance of an election in order to stay in power.

Just as companies aiming for contract renewals need to be planning them from the moment they are first awarded the business, politicians need to be planning their re-election from the moment they first get into power.

That communication must start within the Party itself. At a party conference, therefore, there needs to be an administrative machine in place which will take the key messages which have been identified as the ones which the audience want to know about, and then reinforce them at every stage, from the logos and backdrops to the speeches themselves, from the leaflets on the seats to the press briefings. Issues need to be simplified to make them easy for the audience to grasp, relate to and remember. People also like to know what their government's long term vision is.

It is always comforting to feel that the people in charge know in which direction they are taking us, and this can only be achieved by stating some clear objectives – something else which Thatcher was extremely good at. No-one was ever left in doubt as to how she wanted the Britain of the future to look.

Political personalities

All that we have talked about regarding the projection of personality then comes into play. Although a party must have key, unifying messages in order to win support, individual politicians also have to show that they themselves are capable people, who can be trusted to use power wisely. The public needs to have personalities they can identify with as real people.

Voters can love them or hate them, but they must earn respect. Margaret Thatcher certainly wasn't widely loved, but she was widely respected and made a credible prime minister as a result.

Traditional wisdom suggests that the public does not instinctively trust any politicians – quite the opposite in fact – and any members of parliament who can convince audiences that they truly believe in what they are saying, and that they have the ability and resolve to make it happen, are going to be successful. In any political party there will be a wide divergence of experiences, abilities and philosophies amongst all the top players, and it is the key messages which they are all able to agree on which will win or lose elections for them as a team.

The difficulty for anyone trying to mould these people into a winning team is the very strength of the personalities, their personal ambitions and beliefs. You might construct the most persuasive party message, but if one or two of the senior people in the team speak up with alternative views, you suddenly don't give the appearance of being a team any more.

Any politician who tries to force opinions on other people without asking what they want and genuinely listening to the answers, will fail, just as someone who tries to be all things to all people, and does not identify key issues, will also fail. Governments and oppositions are littered with examples of both these types of politician; the former tend to become maverick visionaries in the wilderness, while the latter lose their credibility by constantly seeming to change course and waffle about subjects on which they are ill-prepared to speak.

Once you have identified the problems or needs, and enunciated them, it is then possible to create a feeling of momentum which will carry a party along. That momentum gives the party the ability to merchandise itself to the constituencies. Many thousands of party workers have to be won over and convinced, because their whole-

hearted commitment is needed if they are to be motivated into putting
in all the hours of work necessary for winning an election.

Television in the Commons

Politics has always involved communications, and television provides
opportunities for politicians to talk to larger audiences more often than
ever before – so why are they so uninspiring, uninteresting and
unattractive to the voting population? Why are they in many cases such
dull speakers?

Television in the House of Commons has been a mixed blessing for
the politicians. For those who are good at presenting themselves it has
been a boon, an opportunity to speak to a far wider audience and to put
their personalities across. On the other side of the coin, however, it has
proved to the general viewing public just how unappealing the vast
majority of members are in terms of what they say and how they say it.

Given that politicians are supposed to be professional communicators, and that they are usually voted into power on the strength of what
they say, television has demonstrated just what an appalling job some
of them actually do of communicating.

The viewing public is therefore led to assume that these people will
be voted into government regardless of their personalities, simply on
the strength of their party machine. If there is a safe seat for any
particular party, it will remain safe regardless of the calibre of the
person running for it.

If this is the case, which it demonstrably is in many instances, the
need to get the team effort right becomes all the more crucial, because it
is the key messages, as enunciated by the most senior and high-profile
members of the party, which will make the difference between winning
and losing for many of the individual members.

If anyone wants to become successful in politics in any country in the
world, it is crucial to think about and work on the basic communication
skills. It is such an obvious statement, and yet so few do it. The growing
power of television may force the rest to change their ways.

Yet all politicians believe that they are brilliant communicators.
Recently, one leading politician actually told me that he rarely, if ever,
used a text for a speech. He was surprised when I described a talk which

I had seen him deliver badly from a script two weeks earlier. Together he and I identified several specific future dates when he would have to be scripted because of the sensitivity of the subject matter, yet he was not prepared to admit that his very mediocre delivery could be improved.

Trapped in the written culture

Government ministers, who are after all the ones who do the majority of the communicating, have the support of extremely erudite, highly intelligent civil servants.

But these civil servants are all from a written culture, highly educated in the ways of producing written briefs. The ministers therefore become used to being able to pick up the briefs or speeches which they are given, and just reproducing them verbatim. The result is that people are frequently bored and unable to follow what is being said.

If someone were to translate all the information which is in the briefs, and in the minds of the civil servants, into 'speak-language', and to insert anecdotes and metaphors to illustrate the points and bring them to life, we would be a nation of great orators, instead of producing one or two every half century.

One of the reasons improvement is slow in the UK is because there is a suspicion of professional communications advice. When companies like Saatchis, Lowe Bell Communications and Kingstree become involved with political figures, it is sometimes held up by opposing parties as evidence of manipulation.

The opposite is true. Professional advisers never tell politicians what to say, they merely help to make them more skilled at saying it, at putting their points across clearly and at being understood. Good communication is not manipulation, it is clarification; and clarity makes manipulation harder. It makes the truth more accessible.

In the US a professional approach to communications has long been accepted by the political establishment, and has therefore become part of the national scene. Most political figures in America are good at giving the appearance of being spontaneous and credible. They are good at making points, although less skilled at the sort of combative debating around which the British system has been built.

European politics

The European political scene provides even greater scope for communications improvements. Language and cultural barriers, coupled with administrative red tape, mean that little of any value is said to, or understood by, anyone who is affected by what European politicians do. The possibilities for confusion are endless.

The need for clarity of thought and expression is paramount if anything worthwhile is to emerge from Europe, and if anyone is to make the EEC his or her political career platform.

Diplomatic circles

Diplomats are also in the business of information management. They frequently have to be discreet about certain subjects in the face of fierce questioning, and they often have to show loyalties to causes with which they might not themselves wholly agree.

The whole world saw an example of diplomats under pressure when Iraq invaded Kuwait in 1990, and the Iraqi ambassadors around the world were required to justify the unjustifiable to the media. It is debatable how good a job they did.

To handle this type of work successfully diplomats need to be confident when they are talking, and they need to inspire confidence in those they meet. Much of their work is therefore dependent on spoken communications, and can be improved and honed with careful training.

When business and politics meet

We have often had to prepare business people to appear as expert witnesses at regulatory hearings in Europe, and at congressional and senatorial hearings in America.

There was one case in which one of America's best-known senators from Massachusetts was interviewing one of our clients from the oil industry.

We had spent some time talking to this client about dealing with difficult questions and discussed various interview techniques for use in exactly these circumstances.

About two months after the interview I was in the same client's office, and I asked him how the interview had gone. He passed me a transcript of the proceedings.

The interview started with the Senator interviewing our client in the normal way, but you could see that after three or four questions our client had succeeded in turning the entire process around so that he was interviewing the Senator. By doing that he was exposing the fact that the Senator really hadn't done much homework on the subject at hand.

The only thing that had allowed the Senator to ask any sort of intelligent questions at all was the in-depth briefing which his aides had prepared for him, complete with a list of the questions he should ask.

As soon as our client had put two or three questions to the Senator one of the aides realised what was happening, and the interview was swiftly brought to an end.

KEY POINTS

- No politician should talk without preparation at any time
- Political and business careers can be built on successful projection of strong personalities
- Briefs and speeches need to be turned into speak-language
- Create key team messages and stick to them
- Prepare for re-election upon election
- Make your vision tangible: use colourful examples and illustrations
- Research what the people want to hear about

Part IV:
Using the System to Win New Business

· 24 ·

The New Business Pitch

Winning new business is important in the good times, but it is vital in difficult economic times.

Everyone is having to do more business pitches than in the past, from major auditing and law firms going after new contracts to advertising agencies, public relations companies and engineering firms chasing new clients.

When a major auditing firm pitches for a large blue chip account it may spend over £100,000 on preparation and documentation. It will do an enormous amount of research into the target company. It will spend many hours of the valuable time of senior partners on building the team which will do the pitching and then, if successful, handle the business.

But the real need is to do a thorough job of preparation for the various critical presentations, while limiting the hours of valuable billable time each key team member must divert to the preparation process.

Investing in presentation skills

Getting business pitches right represents an investment, just as advertising and other marketing expenditure is an investment. If a company doesn't invest time and money in winning new business it will be beaten by the competition. It is as simple as that.

These professional people doing the pitching are not traditional sales people in the classic sense, but more and more they are being required to sell themselves and their companies effectively against stiff opposition. They may not be professional sales people, but they are professionals who are having to sell.

It is surprising how ineffective many of them are at it.

It is a skill which can be learned

Some people believe that winning new business is a knack, something which some people are naturally good at and others aren't.

Some believe that they simply have runs of good and bad luck, but in reality it is all based on experience, proper advice and a determination to form the habit of doing the right things.

Even when you do all the right things you can still lose on a totally subjective point, but by approaching the whole process of business development in a professional manner you can increase the odds of winning substantially. Our aim at Kingstree is to get people into the best possible position to win.

Standing out from the crowd

In most cases companies pitching for large business accounts are very competent in their fields, otherwise they wouldn't be invited to pitch. When they give their presentations, however, it is likely that many of them will be indistinguishable from the opposition.

So how does the potential customer make a choice?

The answer is often that the customers find they can remember more of the key points from one of the pitches than the others, and that the personalities of those presenters came over more clearly and strongly as 'people we can do business with'.

Having ascertained that the professional credentials of all the companies are roughly equal, the prospective client can then make subjective decisions on whom it would like to work with.

Although it may be able to see that any of the companies pitching would be professionally competent at handling the business, there are bound to be some preferred individuals who give the impression of being on the same wavelength.

Given that all the presenting companies are competent to handle the business, the challenge becomes less about winning the business, and more about avoiding being eliminated from the race.

Don't try to prove you can do the job

Business prospects know you can do the job, so it would be a waste of time spending the oral presentation trying to convince the potential clients of that fact. If they have any doubts after the presentation they can ask questions.

No getting out of it

There is no way that a company which is serious about winning new business and growing can avoid the need to give face-to-face presentations.

A potential client has to want to work with you, and that will only happen if that client meets you personally, likes you and trusts you.

One client told us that he was very keen on the 'Beer Factor' when employing outside suppliers. We asked what he meant by that.

'Well,' he said, 'when there is a problem I want to be able to go down to the pub with them to talk about it, and then get back to the mainstream of our work.'

That illustrates the importance of getting on with people if you are going to succeed in the business world, and to get on with someone you have to get to know them first. To do that you have to introduce and sell yourself, which can only be done face-to-face.

It may be more comfortable to prepare written documentation, send it off and hope for the best, but that will not provide a short-cut to success. All companies have to make personal contact with potential customers if they want to succeed. No piece of paper on its own can make a sale!

Companies that do decide to take new business pitching seriously may well need outside advice on how to achieve their goals. The earlier they take that advice the better.

You can't start too soon

All too often Kingstree is called in at the last minute because the companies pitching for the business suddenly realize that they are going to fail if they don't get their acts together.

Although we may be able to polish up their techniques a little at a late stage, it is often too late to do enough to win the business.

The moment that a company knows it is going to be pitching for a piece of business, it should start planning the presentation, and taking whatever professional advice it feels is necessary. If we come in at the end, it may have gone too far down the path to make the radical changes needed for success.

If the right advice is given at the beginning of the process, a great deal of pressure can be taken off the key players, and a lot of time can be saved.

Sometimes it is hard for the team actually doing the pitching to stand back from the complexities of the subject in quite the same way as an external adviser can. Whatever business you are in, there is always a danger that you will get so close to your material that you are no longer able to see what are the key points which the recipients will perceive or understand.

The period between the submission of the written proposal document and the day of the presentation can provide the pitching team with valuable opportunities to build a relationship with the prospective client.

Wherever possible the team should be trying to get feedback on the document, and ascertaining if new ideas and angles need to be developed.

The first mistake that many companies make is failure to establish a critical path from the day they receive the invitation to pitch to the day they give the actual presentation.

Right from Day One there should be a plan, complete with timetables, specific assignments and responsibilities.

There should be an overall team leader with the authority to ensure that all members work to the agreed schedule for determining the sales points, preparation of the segments and visual support. Rehearsals must be held as far in advance as possible to allow for adjustments to be made on time.

The good and the bad

We work with one of the world's leading accountancy firms. They recently had three months to prepare themselves for a presentation to win a major piece of auditing business.

The process which they went through in preparing themselves was absolutely professional and rigorous, and guided them down a path which gave them the very best chance of winning that order.

Every single member of the team knew precisely what the key points were that had to be got across.

Each of the segments was structured carefully to adhere to the overall theme which the team wanted to establish in the eyes of the customers, and the rehearsals were efficient and made good use of the team's time.

If each team member is clear about his or her objectives in what to get across to the listeners, it is relatively easy to measure whether or not those objectives are being met.

At the opposite end of the scale, we were recently called in to a client pitching for one of the largest awards ever made in its industry. We were called in on a Thursday evening to work on a pitch to be made the following Wednesday. Our assumption at the time was that as these people were world leaders they would have their story organized and ready to tell.

We arrived on the Friday morning to find that they hadn't even finalized who was going to be on the team. They solved that during the day, and throughout the weekend we worked with them, persuading each member of the team to express ideas clearly and succinctly, and not to include too much material.

By Monday evening the European chairman flew to Britain to sit in on what he thought would be a final run-through, only to find that the segments were still not in good enough shape for him to see.

On the day before the pitch we had to tell one of the directors that if he didn't start paying attention to what we were telling him we would have to recommend that he be taken off the team.

In the event, they rang us on the Friday and told us that they had got through to the next round and had been invited to talk to the board of the potential client the following week.

We saw a run-through of an abbreviated version of the presentation they had made on the Wednesday.

Again, we discovered that in trying to cut five presentations back into three, they had completely lost the thread of the key sales points that had finally come through in the previous presentation, and which had got them this far.

It turned into another late night while we tried to get the messages for each tightened segment back into shape.

They finally won the contract, and there is no doubt that they are highly competent to handle the business. But that approach to preparation made it very difficult for us to say with real assurance that they were going into the presentations with any reasonable chance of winning.

Competitive advantage – be clear in your thinking

In any competitive tender for business, you need to start by analysing why it is that you have been asked to pitch for the business. What is it about your company which is special and which the potential clients believe they may need?

Which firms are likely to be in competition, and what are their strengths as well as their weaknesses?

Right from the beginning you can start to map out the key reasons why you are better than the competition – or at least different. It is these key points of differentiation which will win or lose the business for you.

If someone is planning to buy a car and there are two or three models which would be equally suitable, it will be the small touches and details which will swing the sale – electric windows, perhaps, or a better stereo. Likewise the major airlines, all of whom are selling roughly the same services at roughly the same prices, have to win customers by offering prettier air hostesses or better in-flight food, or above all a better service to the customer from the initial phone call to collecting luggage at the end of the flight.

If we assume that your basic service is the best available, then you are free to concentrate on the dressings which will make it exceptional and memorable. In many cases that will be a question of customer care and making the product or service easier for the client to understand and use – that is exactly the impression which you need to be able to get across early in the presentation, and then reinforce throughout.

Everything should be clearly laid out and easy for the audience to understand and remember.

The potential clients will take it for granted that you are providing sound professional standards of quality and commitment, otherwise you wouldn't be there.

All your competitors will be offering these basics as well. So what you need to do is find the small details which are relevant – perhaps one of your team has specific experience of the potential client's industry, or you have developed a particularly user-friendly system of weekly client reports, or a new method of working that will cut costs – and pull them out to the front of the presentation.

It will be these details which win the business – provided they are details that the client wants to hear about.

Don't be deceived

If you have worked out the best way to present your key messages to a client, don't be deceived by appearances into returning to traditional methods.

Just because the potential customer has a hi-tech boardroom doesn't mean that you have to produce an electronic presentation which uses all its equipment – unless you honestly believe that is the best way of achieving your goals.

If a client seems very formal, there is no reason why you should pretend to be equally formal just to win the business, unless such a style comes naturally to you.

If you do change your personality in that way you will seem insincere to start with; and if you are successful, you will have won the business under false pretences – which means you risk losing it pretty quickly afterwards.

Avoid numbers

There is often a tendency when going for new business to make the presentation numbers-driven, filled with facts and figures to prove that you know your business. That isn't necessarily what the potential client wants to hear about.

If the figures are highly relevant you might decide to give them out in written form at the end, or in the proposal document which you put in at the initial stage of the operation. But if you simply talk through a series of figures with the audience, either you are going to lose their attention because they don't understand what you are talking about, or you will bore them because they have heard it all before.

If the audience really needs to know more detail they will ask questions at the end.

With all the high technology developments in visual aids systems, some people feel that they should be demonstrating that they use the most up-to-date technology, even if there is no real need for it to support the key messages.

Visual aids are only useful if they support the case being put. If they are used gratuitously they frequently act as a distraction. Many new business pitches are won in spite of visual aids, rather than because of them.

In our view, all presentations should be capable of running independently of any visual aids. On a practical level that means that if there is a disaster and your carousel of slides jams, or your computer goes wrong, you can still go ahead with the presentation.

It also imposes a discipline which ensures that no-one short-cuts on preparation, believing that some slick visual aids will cover up the gaps.

Put yourself in the recipient's place

One very good question to ask yourself is: 'if I were sitting on this panel, looking at four different companies selling the same goods in one day, what sort of things would I like and dislike? What will be memorable and what won't?'

A common mistake which presenting companies make is to put too much information into the oral presentation. They feel they have to provide every single fact and figure which supports their bid for the work. The more complex the message is, the more impressed they think the client will be.

This is completely wrong. Complex material should be presented in written form, or in the question and answer sessions.

In an oral presentation you are just putting across the key points and your personality.

Holding the attention of the audience

The presenters must therefore not lose the attention of any of the members of the audience from the moment they start to the moment they finish.

If we can make sure that happens, then the key points of the speakers' messages will automatically stick in the audience's minds, and their professional competence will be reinforced in the client's eyes as their positive personality characteristics emerge.

If you fail to keep the attention of every member of a buying panel and one vital member of the audience (even the most junior), has been unable to understand something that you have said, or has missed an important point because his attention wandered at the critical moment and he has been unable to follow the argument from there on, you have run an unnecessary risk of elimination.

It is possible, for instance, that this person has a question which he or she is dying to ask during the question and answer period, but, human nature being what it is, can't speak up through fear of looking stupid by asking about something which everyone else has been able to grasp, or which might have been covered during a lapse in his attention.

If that has happened it means there is at least one person who could well justify voting against you when the time comes, simply on the grounds that you failed to control his attention, and therefore left one or more issues unresolved in his mind.

If you know how to avoid being eliminated that is a first step in moving into position to win.

Create a strong leader

There is always a need for a strong team leader at any pitch, but during the actual presentation itself that leader must be seen to delegate questions to the team, and allow or even encourage everyone on the team to participate.

That will result in an elevation of the leader's position, because he will be seen to be at the top of a strong team, and will show the client that there is strength in depth.

If it is a major contract, the clients are not going to want to award it to one person, in case that person leaves the company or becomes ill, or simply doesn't have time to handle the day-to-day business.

It is vital, however, that everyone who presents is actually going to be on the team which will be handling the client's business. In the past it has been the habit of many companies to have their top executives pitching for business and, once it is won, never being seen again.

Who is going to speak has to be decided on factors like seniority, expertise and who will need exposure to the client. Business is frequently lost simply because the chemistry is wrong between the main presenter and the potential client.

You will be able to form an idea at initial meetings of who is going to get on best with the potential client. They will be the ones who will be put to work on the account if it is won, and they should be the ones doing the talking at the presentation. That way the presenting company can say to the client 'what you see is what you get', which is a powerful selling statement.

For that to work, however, it is important that the presenters are showing their true personalities when they are speaking. Sometimes the pressure of the situation might make them seem withdrawn or pompous when they are actually the opposite.

If this is the case, then they need to be coached in how to put across their true personalities in a relaxed, confident way, otherwise the client may end up buying – or not buying – for the wrong reasons.

Don't overload the team

If a potentially large contract is at stake, senior managers are often tempted to join the pitching team, even though they have nothing direct to contribute.

There is no point in the company chairman coming along to the presentation unless he has something to contribute. The potential client will no doubt be pleased to meet him, but will then wonder why he sits silently while others do the presenting, or else why the chairman has to do his own selling. However there are occasions when it is important for the chairman to participate and to demonstrate the importance you are according to their business.

Similarly, if you are going after an international account, there is sometimes a temptation to fly someone over from America, someone else from Japan and a few people from Europe, and wheel them all in to meet the client and demonstrate the international capabilities of the company.

It serves no useful purpose at all; the client feels swamped by people, and might well wonder how all of them have the time to get on planes to chase round the world after a single piece of business which is by no means a certainty.

The only people on a pitching team should be the ones who have something solid to contribute.

Cutting down the complexity

The next mistake that many new business presenters make is to make the pitch far too complex.

The problem with all new business presentations, whether by an engineering company or a financial institution, is that the presenters often know their subject very well indeed. This immediately opens up a communications gap between the 'expert' doing the talking and the 'generalist' doing the listening.

If a technical engineer has just designed a new core for an aircraft engine, he can go on speaking about the specifications of the product for hours, with very few other people able to understand what he is talking about. Yet there are many things which an audience of potential customers would want to know about a subject like that.

The key is to cut down the number of points which you intend to make, and to look for the customer benefits rather than the features of whatever you are selling.

Getting the balance right

The mistaken view of many presenters, particularly when dealing with technical or financial subjects, is that for a presentation to be weighty it has to be stacked with details. That ignores the fact that everyone in the audience has a different level of understanding of the subject.

The vital issue is what is actually happening in the minds of the listeners. People who are paying attention will take a particular piece of information as the presenter speaks it, process it internally and compare it to what they already know about the subject. Then they come back to the presenter for more information or the next point. By definition this means the communication is 'two-way', in the sense that both speaker and listener are actively participating in it.

To somebody hearing this information for the first time and with no background knowledge, everything the presenter says will be a revelation, provided it is kept simple and illustrated with concrete examples.

The fear is that if you keep it simple for these people you will sound patronizing to the ones who do have some background knowledge.

In reality nothing could be further from the truth. The expert in the audience is merely validating each point that the speaker is making in his own mind, ensuring that it is correct, and filling in any gaps through his own knowledge and experience. So the two different people will effectively be hearing two different presentations.

It's not what you say

Again we return to the idea that it is not what you say that is all-important, it is what the audience thinks about what you are saying that is critical. That will be based on their own previous knowledge of the subject, and their ability to process what you are saying.

This problem will often befall speakers at new business pitches because of the mix of people they are likely to have in their audience.

Some of them will be there because of their technical knowledge of the subject, and they will understand everything that is being said, whether it is about engineering or finance. Others will be generalists and may have no idea about the detail of the subject.

In many cases it is the generalists who are the most senior members of the audience, and they are the ones who sign the cheques and make the decisions about whether to hire a firm or not. But these generalists probably rely on the advice of the specialists as to which of the pitching companies sounds as if it really knows what it is talking about.

The speakers therefore have to demonstrate a grasp of the subject which will convince the other experts in the room, while still making the messages clear enough for the generalists to understand.

The answer is to go in somewhere in the middle, proving to the experts that you have a good grasp of the subject, without going into too much detail, and raising illustrations in their minds which they recognize as being things of which they themselves have had experience. Here the goal may be to provide a series of questions which will allow the presentation team to demonstrate the depth of their knowledge of the subject.

While the experts are relating what you have said to their own experience, the generalists are listening to what you are saying and thinking 'that's interesting, I didn't know that'.

If you are going to err on either side of this fine dividing line it is always better to err on the side of over-simplification as opposed to over-complexity.

Summarize

Another way to ensure that everyone is keeping up with you is to stop and summarize every so often, using analogies or examples that everyone can understand. This is particularly valid if you have just said something relatively lengthy and technical.

Say, for instance, you have just delivered some technical information on why your aircraft are the best on the market, but you know there are some non-technical people in the audience. All you have to do is pause, and say; 'The points I am making are: we make the 'planes stronger, we make them fly faster, and we make them more fuel-efficient'. You can then move on to the next point.

A real example of that happened with one of our aircraft manufacturing clients. They were explaining why one of their 'planes had to have a longer undercarriage than rivals did. The reason was that the 'plane had a longer fuselage, and unless the undercarriage was also longer the tail would hit the deck on take-off.

Having stated that fact they were able to go into the technical aspects of the hydraulics systems, but before going on to the next subject they repeated the key reason, which was to stop the 'plane's tail dragging on the runway. It was a very clear image which everyone could understand, and it explained the problem exactly.

At the end of your talk you expect the audience to come away with two or three key points. You want them to understand the shape of the whole forest, but you want them specifically to remember three or four of the trees which make up that forest. The technical people will need to have those 'trees' justified to them if they are going to believe in them.

Cut down the talking time

We have found that many companies choose to spend 50 minutes of the hour scheduled for a typical new business presentation talking, leaving ten minutes for questions and answers.

In most cases this would be a mistake. It would probably be better to talk for about twenty minutes – which is as long as most people can concentrate – and leave the rest open for questions. That way you create a full two-way flow and allow the personalities on both sides to interact and get to know one another.

At the beginning of the meeting the leader can inform the audience that this is going to happen, so that they aren't taken by surprise by an abrupt end to the presentation.

There will always be questions if you have pitched the presentation right. If you have made it too complex people may be afraid to speak up in case they demonstrate their ignorance or ask about something which was covered but they didn't hear.

There may also be internal politics at work within the potential client company, with people asking difficult questions in order to elevate themselves in the eyes of their colleagues in the room. Provided the presenters have done their preparation, however, and are clear on what their key points are, they will not be caught out.

When answering questions beware of over-answering. Always be crisp and to the point, and don't be led off on a ramble into related or unrelated areas.

We all have a tendency to over-answer questions, partly due to the amount of specialist knowledge we carry in our heads, and partly due to a desire to be helpful. But there is nothing more off-putting to questioners than to receive another mini-presentation with every answer.

It is important to be seen to be someone who can think on one's feet and be clear and concise in one's responses.

Constant practice but less rehearsal

It is easy for me or any of my colleagues to put these points across to presenters when we are advising them. But, as with developing any skill to championship level, they need continual practice if they are to become second nature.

That does not mean that speakers should rehearse a presentation until they are word-perfect. It is important to retain the spontaneity of a new business pitch, to demonstrate that you are talking from a deep-rooted knowledge of your subject and with a good understanding of the potential client's needs. If you are too well-rehearsed it will begin to sound like a script, and you will become wooden.

If you have learnt your words off by heart – or nearly done so – you are also in danger of panicking if you then feel your memory is letting you down.

During any rehearsals, it will be helpful if you can persuade colleagues to ask you some genuine questions – as difficult as possible – so that you get an idea of how it is going to be when you are in the real situation.

It is not constructive, however, to have a lot of people from your own company constantly pulling your presentation to pieces. Everyone has different opinions on how a case should be put, many of them completely at variance, and if you listen to all of them you are likely to end up unable to say anything at all.

Cutting out the corporatese

My colleague Alistair Grant was called in by the chairman of a large multi-national company because, the chairman complained, one of his executives was the most monotonous and boring speaker imaginable. He wanted Alistair to do something about it.

Alistair went to meet the executive and started talking to him about general subjects. He discovered that the man wasn't monotonous at all, he was actually very animated. Without revealing what he was doing, Alistair switched on the camera and recorded their conversation.

He then asked the executive to stand up and deliver his speech from notes and, as the chairman had predicted, he became monotonous and boring.

The difference between the two recordings was very simple. On the first informal recording, he was talking in everyday English, but as soon as he started to talk from his notes he went into 'corporatese' language, using phrases like:

'I must advise you that we need to proceed with caution because this subject is confidential and it would be inappropriate at this moment in time to discuss it with others without first gaining clearance through the right channels', when what he meant was: 'This is a sensitive subject, so don't talk about it outside this room unless you have checked with me first.'

Preparing for a pitch

When we first go to see clients who are preparing for a new business pitch, we want to hear from them what they think their competitive advantage is, what the angle is that they think will win them the business.

The process then evolves from that initial meeting to the actual presentation itself. Kingstree runs the rehearsals, checking any visual aids to ensure that they are complementary and not distracting, and taking any members of the team who haven't undergone training by us in the past through an accelerated scheme to prepare them for their roles.

Although everyone should be as natural as possible, any new business pitch is a piece of theatre, which should be stage-managed in the same way as a play. People need to know where they will be sitting, what order they will be speaking in, and what their parts in the plot are.

The pitching team needs to know in advance the lay-out of the room they are going to be presenting in, so that they can assess the best way to place everyone. Most potential clients would be happy to describe or show the room to the project manager of a pitching company.

It is also quite reasonable to ask the potential client what it is expecting of the pitching team. Will they, for instance, be talking to two or three people in a boardroom, or to 20 from a stage? How much time is being allocated? Who will be present, and are they expecting a specific number of people on the pitching team? Are they expecting visual aids?

It is also reasonable to make your own preferences known. If there is a choice of rooms, or styles of presentation, you can let the potential clients know, so that they can make the necessary preparations. Do you prefer to give your pitch standing or sitting, for instance?

Final rehearsal

The final rehearsal will preferably be about a week before the actual presentation. In that last run-through our job is to vet all the elements and techniques for maximum effectiveness and impact.

At a rehearsal you should ensure that the whole team arrives with their completed notes and any visual aids that they want to use. Then you can discuss things like seating arrangements and timings for each speaker. At this stage you also need to check that the links between the speakers are smooth and logical.

Although you need a strong leader it must be clear during the presentation that it is a team effort, and no single personality should be allowed to dominate the proceedings. If one person is too strong the clients will get the impression that they are dealing with a one-man band, and that will make them nervous about the quality and calibre of the supporting team.

Be aware that there is no such thing as an even playing field when you are making competitive pitches. You may never know exactly what is going on in the minds of the audience sitting in front of you. It is possible that they are only holding the 'beauty contest' in order to persuade the incumbent to reduce its fees. Or they may have made their minds up about who gets the job even before they hear your pitch, and are simply going through the motions out of politeness or because they wish to be seen to do a thorough search.

But, win or lose, the experience of pitching under pressure is always much too valuable to miss.

On the day, you should arrive looking enthusiastic and confident about the project, and stay alert throughout the proceedings. It is also vital to pay attention to your colleagues' remarks as if it were the first time you have heard it all.

This may seem obvious, but a number of our clients have described pitches that went wrong because members of the team appeared bored or disinterested while other members were talking.

Have a permanent new business pitching capability

The one point which keeps recurring as we work on competitive new business pitches is the vital importance of initiating a well-disciplined critical path governing each event in the preparation process.

Consistently successful new-business teams all focus the responsibility on one or two senior individuals who manage and co-ordinate each phase of the pitch process, maintaining rigid discipline in ensuring that all key participants attend relevant meetings and work to a sensible timetable.

The single biggest mistake in organizing teams who make competitive tenders is allowing the process to be de-centralized, with each relevant department working on its own and co-ordination and rehearsal being left to the last minute.

Yet this is exactly what occurs in many service businesses. The excuse that is always offered is that the individuals who have been selected are 'too busy working for existing clients' to dedicate the time and effort required to mount an effective campaign.

If this is true, then how will they be able to handle the increased workload should they win the competitive pitch?

Our experience suggests that this excuse is nonsense.

Professionals who sell

We are entering an age where people who would never have dreamed that they might function as salespeople are having to get out there to present their cases to potential clients.

These presenters fall into two main categories; 'Professional salespeople' and 'Professionals who can also sell'.

While the former see themselves as salespeople, with the primary role of selling, the latter think of themselves first and foremost as professionals. At the same time, however, they know they are going to have to demonstrate the abilities of their firms and themselves to prospective clients, and to develop additional business from their clients. In virtually all the organizations we serve it is the people who generate business who receive the greatest recognition and reward.

Don't stay to lunch

After the presentation is over you may be invited to have drinks or even lunch with the potential client – DON'T DO IT.

It may sound like a good opportunity to get to know the clients better, but it is actually an opportunity for you to undo completely the good work which you may have done in the presentation itself.

Whereas in the presentation you were thoroughly prepared and rehearsed, and clear in your minds what your key messages were, when you relax over lunch you are quite likely to waffle about subjects which you have not researched thoroughly, and you may even raise doubts in the client's mind about just how competent you are.

One major office product company trains its staff to leave a customer's office the moment a sale is made. They are told not even to wait for the lift but to head straight down the stairs – because those few seconds or minutes can provide the time for second thoughts.

Stick with the winning issues

Once you have identified the key points, or winning issues, then you must stay with them.

Get every member of the team to think about them and add flesh to them. The challenge remains to win your audience's attention, and then to keep it throughout.

The actual buying decision might not be made until two days or even two weeks after the presentation, so it is vital that the audience is able to remember what the key points were.

There are no hard or fast rules about the format which you use, but the most popular is notes, which will keep you on track and ensure that you don't miss out any key points or stray off at a tangent.

You need to start strongly – preferably with your key messages. You must resist covering too many points and using too many examples and illustrations – generally only one per point otherwise you will dilute your message once again.

Use pauses, as we have explained before, to show that you are thinking about what you are saying, and to give time for your messages to sink in.

Remember – you do not need to make any change to your normal style of delivery in order to give a presentation. The closer you can be to your normal personality the better.

Just as you started on a high note you should also end strongly by summarizing again all the key points of what you are actually bringing to the party – points that differentiate you from your competitors. Don't be afraid to close the presentation by asking for the order, letting the client know that you really do want the business.

KEY POINTS

- You do not need to prove you can do the job
- Stick to the winning issues
- Be yourself – no style change
- Pause for memorability
- Summarize to give signposts
- Don't overload the team
- Build on your team strengths
- Start preparing as early as possible
- Avoid numbers
- Get as much information in advance about the client as possible
- Pitches are lost by people not companies

· 25 ·

One-to-One Selling Situations

There is a wealth of published material available for the training of sales people, much of which teaches them how to interact with their prospects, and how to present themselves effectively with the back-up of sales literature and other aids, all boiling down to the simple dictum, 'know your customer'.

It is well recognized that few people will buy any product or service until they feel a sense of trust in the sales person and his organization. That feeling of trust begins to develop when the sales person shows a real interest in and concern for the customer's needs.

Against that background, you still come up against the same spoken communications problems as in any other area of business.

Selling appointments

Those problems start when you try to make the initial appointment with the prospect. Whatever you are selling, whether it is a new car, a consulting service, or a new type of potato crisp, at your first contact you are normally trying to sell an appointment.

From that moment everything that you say will count for or against you, and will help or hinder you in the final winning of the sale.

If you appear nervous and unsure of yourself when describing the product, the prospect is going to draw certain conclusions about its quality, and the quality of a company which sends out someone who doesn't seem to know what he is talking about.

To give too much information will annoy and bore prospects while too little will leave them puzzled and unwilling to take a risk. Evasive answers to questions will undermine the prospect's trust in the sales person, as will too much repetition.

In the end people buy from people first, not from companies. Provided the company is supplying a product or service which is competitive, the final choice of who to buy from will depend on the personal chemistry of seller and buyer. If customers like and trust someone, then they will do business with that person.

By honing spoken communications skills it is possible to influence how prospects think of you.

Use illustrations

One of the asset management companies with whom we work was going to sell its services to a major US municipal pension fund. It was by far the smallest player, competing with giant financial institutions. On paper it didn't stand a chance, and was lucky to have been included in the find round.

As we waited to begin a rehearsal, the head of the company was telling me about his new Saab car. He had been into the garage a few months before and had been looking at Saab's new models. He had been impressed, but he had decided that the gear mechanism didn't suit him, the boot was too small and there wasn't room in the back for all his children, so he told the salesman he would look at other models.

A week later the salesman from the Saab garage had rung him up to say that a new model was just out, and he thought it addressed the problems which had worried my client.

Sure enough, the gear change was smoother, the boot was larger and the rear seats offered more room, so my client bought the car. After the first service he got another call from the salesman checking that he was entirely happy with everything. 'That,' he said to me, 'is what I call good salesmanship and on-going service.'

'Why don't you tell that story when you pitch for the pension fund's business,' I suggested, 'and explain that that is exactly the sort of service which you give to your customers.'

He took my advice and they actually won that piece of business, against all the competitors who provided vast amounts of detail on their financial strategies. The reason, I believe, was that everyone on the panel was able to identify with that story.

They took it for granted that the company knew its business when it came to asset management because they had read the proposal documentation, but they wanted to be sure that they were hiring a company that would know how to give them good service once they had been selected.

The listeners were able to picture exactly what the man was talking about and relate it to their own experience, and it stuck in their memories.

Keep it simple

Whatever product you are selling, whether it is a power station, an office chair or a financial service, it is crucial to keep it simple and not to overload your listeners with information and details which may be interesting, but which don't contribute directly to the points you need to make.

Start by giving a round-up of the benefits of the product (as broad as possible), and then allow the potential customers to ask questions. If they are interested in the technical details of how the product works, then they will ask. If they are not interested then there is no point in confusing the picture by telling them.

Successful telephone selling

Everyone has to use the telephone at some stage, usually at the critical moment of making appointments. The impression that your voice gives is the only clue which the listener has as to whether to give up some valuable time to meet you face-to-face, or indeed whether to buy from you directly over the 'phone.

He or she is going to be making value judgements, whether

consciously or not, from the first words that you speak right to the end of the conversation.

There are a number of right and wrong ways to use the telephone, and a number of books and courses are dedicated to teaching telephone techniques.

But, from a communications viewpoint, the principles are clear. Anyone using the 'phone for a sales contact must listen more than talk.

Someone speaking on the 'phone needs to have the key points of the message well defined before starting the call, but must not stick rigidly to one pre-defined course. The message must be sufficiently flexible to provide the option of selecting different paths to reflect comments and signals from the prospect.

Again, the trick is to listen acutely for indications from the other person, and to avoid gabbling through a list of points, barely drawing a breath, and allowing precious little time for the prospect to digest each idea before moving on.

Because you do not have the advantage of being able to read the expressions on a listener's face when talking over the 'phone, you have to be even more aware of the effect of pauses and of the words to use.

The best approach generally involves asking questions which suggest you have some knowledge of the prospect's business. This will encourage the prospect to talk about himself and his company, and you will be able to pick up clues as to how to proceed.

You should produce just enough information to interest the listener, remembering that you are just one of many calls going to that individual in any working day, but not enough to make him think he has heard it all and need not find out any more.

Getting past the gatekeepers

The more senior the person is, the more likely that he or she will have a 'gatekeeper' in the form of a secretary or personal assistant, whose job it is to screen out the calls which the boss does not want to take.

To deal with this you must have done enough research beforehand to have at your fingertips enough information to persuade the gatekeeper to let you through.

If you call early in the morning or late in the evening and are consequently able to get straight through to your target, you must immediately be able to excite his interest.

So once again you need to start by saying exactly who you are and within the first few seconds state your key message. There is nothing more annoying when you are busy than having someone rambling without getting to the point.

The same principles apply as those for writing business letters, in which if you don't attract attention within the first paragraph the reader will not bother to continue. Newspaper journalists use the same approach.

Before you start to dial, you should analyse exactly what you hope to achieve with the call. In many cases it will just be the making of an appointment. That means telling the listener just enough to excite his interest, but not enough to make him feel that he doesn't need to hear any more.

As in any live presentation, you also need to know when to stop talking and allow silence to occur to make the other person talk. You must then let him have his say.

As soon as the listener has agreed to whatever you asked, you should stop talking immediately. It is surprising how many people, even after a prospect has said 'yes', will continue to the bitter end of their sales script, demonstrating that they are not listening and not thinking. By the time they finish it is quite likely the prospect will have changed his mind and will be saying 'no'.

Client care

The telephone is also a useful tool for client care programmes. Once someone has bought a product or service there are endless opportunities to call and enquire how things are going, and to elicit information from customers as to whether they are ready to buy again or up-grade.

It is always easier to sell something to an existing customer than to find a new one, yet the majority of companies concentrate all their efforts on the pursuit of new leads, and pay scant attention to the best potential source of new business – their existing client-base.

Every call, however, must have a distinct purpose to it – a key message – which should be stated quickly and succinctly, so that clients continue to be happy to receive the calls and do not feel pestered.

KEY POINTS

- Sell appointments, not services
- Customers don't always want detail
- Help them picture the product benefits
- Listen more than you talk
- Make your message flexible

· 26 ·

Presenting Creative Ideas to Non-Creative Audiences

We do a lot of work for major advertising agencies and other creative businesses such as public relations consultancies and design firms. Most of our briefs centre around new business pitches because that is where the creative industry has the greatest trouble in putting its ideas across to potential clients.

What constantly surprises us is how bad these highly creative people are at making creative presentations of their own skills. During the 80s many of these companies grew very large through acquisition, but there has been surprisingly little investment in skills training, particularly presentation skills.

Their business is communications, yet they approach the whole question of preparing new business pitches and actual presentations very badly and amateurishly. Often it is simply that they do not approach the project systematically, as they would if they were performing one of their normal services for an existing client, eg. putting together a media strategy.

Every week in *Campaign*, the advertising industry's trade journal, there are stories of agencies working throughout nights and weekends to get their pitches ready by a deadline. They seem to wear their inefficiency as a badge of office, as if it demonstrates a kind of professional machismo. Perhaps they believe that it shows how much they care about winning the account, and demonstrates how hard they will work on it once they have secured the business.

In reality what they are demonstrating is that they can't organize their own marketing and communications efforts properly. So why should the client company entrust them with theirs?

It may not be 'all right on the night'

Because they are mostly very self-confident and successful people, they seem to assume that it will all come together on the day. Many believe that a sense of urgency and panic will stimulate their creative juices, making their abilities shine through, and as a result they will somehow manage to win the business. This is absolutely not the way to go about things. Perhaps it was in the past, but it certainly isn't today.

It is also a mistake to think that this helter-skelter approach demonstrates that they are creative people. Actors are also creative people, but they would not think of going on stage or film set without having thought through what they were going to do, studied their lines, and taken advice from professionals like producers, directors, costume and set designers and stage managers.

Behind every successful creative endeavour there must be a steely professionalism which provides a structure within which the creativity can flourish.

Listen before you talk

Many advertising agencies demonstrate their arrogance the moment a potential client rings up to enquire about their services. The first thing they will normally do is invite the enquirer into the agency for a 'credentials presentation'. The client duly arrives and the agency people then talk 'at' him, telling him how great the agency is and showing examples of work done for other clients.

What they should be doing is what everyone in the selling business knows, which is asking the caller questions about his business, and studying his problems and needs, so that the agency can demonstrate its understanding of what issues need to be addressed.

That way the agency team can begin to demonstrate how, with an understanding of the client's problems, they will formulate solutions, and they can begin to form a relationship with the potential client, even at that early stage.

Most clients have made enough preliminary enquiries to establish that an agency has the right credentials before making the initial 'phone call. They know that the agency is equipped to do the creative work; what they are looking for is people who will endeavour to understand their business and with whom they will be able to work.

There are often many millions of pounds worth of business riding on creative pitches. They therefore deserve to be looked at very seriously, and approached in an organized, business-like way.

The moment that an enquiry comes in over the telephone or through the post, someone should be starting to plan how the business is going to be won. A schedule should be prepared which allows the final rehearsals to take place several days before the pitch itself, leaving plenty of time for each stage of the operation to be handled professionally (see Chapter 24 on new business pitches).

Any agency chiefs that I have called to task on this subject give standard excuses of being too busy to set up a system, and having too many commitments on behalf of other clients.

How can this be so? If they can spare the time to do the job badly at the last minute, they can spare time to do it effectively a few weeks before. If they have a properly organized system in place they will actually be saving themselves a good deal of time, as well as winning more business.

A personality business

All service industries rely very largely on personalities. If the client doesn't like the team of people handling its public relations or design account, for instance, then those people will lose the business.

The two sides need to get to know one another as soon as possible, (a) to avoid wasting one another's time and (b) so that the one pitching for the business can impress the potential client with the strength of its convictions and its other personality traits.

If is therefore critical that those personality traits come across right from the beginning – which brings us back to the notion of being yourself at all times and projecting your personality.

If the clients like and trust the team that is working on the account, then they are more likely to give a sympathetic hearing to any ideas or schemes which the team comes up with and which might need 'selling' to the client by the creative team.

The trap which many creative people fall into in the business world is giving the impression that they believe in some way that they are superior to the clients they serve. It is a sort of professional arrogance which can arise in any industry which requires a degree of specialist knowledge – from garage mechanics to solicitors, bankers to doctors.

Designers have been particularly guilty of this in recent years, tending to assume that their way of doing things is the right way and anyone who questions it is quite simply wrong.

That sort of attitude can work for some people for a short time, when they are right at the top of their profession, but it very soon backfires. People do not like being made to feel inadequate and they dislike those who make them feel that way. They are more likely to look for ways to cut the culprits down to size – which may mean rejecting their ideas or even sacking them.

In all the creative professions there is a tendency for people to dress differently and behave differently from the majority of the clients that they serve. Sometimes by doing so they are sending out the wrong messages to those clients before they even open their mouths. When they do open their mouths they are quite likely to compound the error.

Cut out speculative creative work

There is a growing and, in our opinion, healthy movement amongst agencies to refuse to do creative work specifically for a pitch. For one thing it is extremely expensive to do in terms of man-hours, but it is also an inefficient way of going after new business.

The chances are that because of the limited timeframe of the pitch the work will not be the best that the agency could do under normal circumstances. But no matter how good it is, it will still be a lottery as to who wins. It will still depend on whether the prospective customers happen to like the creative approach presented that day, or whether they prefer a competitor's.

Either way, it is irrelevant. Prospective clients should be basing the buying judgement on whether they think the company is competent to handle the business from its past creative record, and whether they think that the agency team are the sort of people that they would be happy working with.

The agency presentation – and this does not just apply to advertising, but to film makers, public relations consultants, designers and all the rest – should therefore put across the key points which the pitching team think are important to the prospective client, not merely aim to convey an impression of competence and creativity, because that will happen anyway.

If the team can show that they are sympathetic to the client's problems, and capable of identifying what the problem is, they should be given the job. Coming up with an instant creative decision is not the answer, and is a waste of everyone's resources.

Increased effort results in increased rewards

The trend in many sectors of business at the moment is for clients to make it harder for suppliers to win their business, but then to stay with them for longer. There is therefore more at stake in every new business pitch, and it becomes ever more critical to increase the percentage of pitches which succeed.

The trick of success, particularly if there are to be a series of presentations before the agency gets to the final stage at which the business is awarded, is to provide a consistency of approach. Agencies need to make it clear to potential customers what the individual strengths of the team members are, because it is those perceptions which will prove decisive when an agency is finally selected.

If you leave preparation to the last moment it is unlikely that you will be consistent in the messages you are putting out or in your success rate. You will also field a team consisting of a number of individuals standing up to speak without preparation and without any consistency of message from the team as a whole.

If a team is made up of creative people it can sometimes be difficult to persuade them to conform to a team message. But it is vital that they do so.

If someone finds it impossible to do this, but is so brilliant creatively that the company can't afford to let him go, then he should be introduced to the potential clients informally – with credentials – but should be kept away from any formal presentation teams.

With no consistency of message it is impossible for the listeners to go away with the key points fixed in their minds. It is also impossible for them to be sure what the approach of the team to handling their business is going to be.

Will it be more like that of the first speaker, or the last? They need to be able to identify a consistent theme or thread to the strategy which is being put forward.

A permanent new business handling capacity

Any firm which is serious about winning more pitches must appoint a new business director. Once appointed he or she should be given the status within the organization to make sure that the right people turn up to the right meetings and prepare themselves well in advance.

In many cases it requires an internal selling job to convince people that a percentage of their time has to be devoted to on-going new business activities. Any company which has not developed that sort of culture will eventually have problems.

If any maufacturing company was run along the lines of the average advertising agency or public relations consultancy – at least in terms of how they approach selling – they would be out of business very quickly.

In the past, the creative industries would have laughed at the idea that they should have systems and processes like the industrial world. These days they can't afford to be so high-handed. Advertising and public relations are not arcane arts, they are processes in the marketing chain, and they should be treated as such.

In every agency and consultancy, therefore, there should be a Presentation Development Process laid down for use from the time that an enquiry first comes in, with a critical path mapped out to the day of presentation and beyond, into the follow-up phase.

The more time between these two dates the better, as long as you are using that time effectively by ticking off the boxes along the critical path as you reach certain stages, from the composition of the team to an initial strategy meeting, to assigning tasks and on to final rehearsals.

One person ought to be responsible for the progress of the project, and needs the authority to push it along.

KEY POINTS

- Be systematic, do not leave success to chance
- Listen to clients' problems before boasting about your achievements
- Isolate key points and place them against an impression of competence and creativity
- Be consistent in your message
- Don't sell your skills with arrogance
- Don't create unnecessary barriers to understanding through dress and appearance

· 27 ·

Talking in Foreign Tongues

The Kingstree system works in other western languages just as well as in English, because there are consistencies in the characteristics of normal spoken communication in all the major western languages and cultures.

While there are distinct differences in the interpretation of so-called 'body language', the basic elements of receiver-driven spoken interchange remain.

When Salomon Brothers in London were handling financing for the German Federal Railway, they asked us to advise the two senior executives who were coming over to speak.

They were the chairman and the finance director, and the latter was particularly concerned that his English wasn't good enough for the presentation.

The chairman declined to see us, believing that he did not need any advice, although he agreed to allow us to edit his speech to make it more conversational.

The finance director, however, was very happy to receive any help we could give him. Our consultant went to see him in Germany for two sessions.

When it came to the presentation the chairman stood up and talked off the cuff, letting the ideas come to him spontaneously with only a loose structure.

The finance director then stood up and delivered his speech concisely and effectively, as if he had been speaking English all his life.

Because he had realized that he needed help he had been willing to listen, and had then rigidly followed the Kingstree System for delivering a script (although in his case it was a script in a language with which he was unfamiliar).

After the presentation the chairman of Salomon's, John Gutfreund, came up to me. He had already been through our programme and he also knew that we had only been able to reach one of the two executives.

'Well, Lee,' he said, 'no doubt which of them was your client. But then,' he paused, 'the other one *is* the chairman.'

To which I could only reply; 'Yes, Chairman.'

Crossing the Atlantic

People often joke about the British and Americans being 'divided by a common language', but it is certainly true in many ways. Not only are there actual words which have different connotations on either side of the Atlantic, but there are innumerable cultural differences in the way we behave.

While visitors working in another country should always be aware of the rules regarding etiquette in the host culture, they should also not be afraid to remain 'themselves', otherwise they run the risk of appearing insincere and becoming completely ineffective.

One of our clients is a major international credit card company. A new manager was hired for the UK and Ireland office, which represented a major sector of the company's business but was producing a low proportion of the company's profits.

When this young man arrived he turned out to be a very aggressive and energetic American. He had been working for the company for some time, and his assessment of what needed to be done was a major shake-up in the responsibilities of some of the key people, possibly with some lay-offs and cut-backs.

Right from the beginning he needed to establish his own credibility and style of management. But at every turn, right down to the way he ran his staff meetings in London, he was continually being frustrated by people saying, 'but that isn't the way we do things here'.

He knew that if he didn't impose his style of management onto the company, the objectives which had been set for him were not going to be met.

He came to us and told us his problems. He was a very straightforward man, always speaking his mind and absolutely clear in his definition of the goals and objectives for which the company should be aiming.

Our suggestion was that he should impose that sort of rigorous discipline on the organization.

The best way to do that, we suggested, was to start the next meeting at which everyone gathered by stating his case clearly, hitting them right between the eyes with the key point – 'I have been sent here to achieve these things: the way we are going to do that is as follows'.

He should, we suggested, use exactly the same sort of language that he was using to us, and he should make it crystal clear to everybody what was expected of them, so that there could be no mystery about it.

Initially he was sceptical, because it flew in the face of all the things which his British advisers had been telling him. But we insisted that even if he tried to adapt his own protective colouring to the British jungle, he would never come across as anything other than what he was, a forceful, American-trained manager.

If he tried to change his personal style he would be seen to be phoney, and in addition he wouldn't get the job done. In the event he took the advice and has been very successful as a result.

The cultural barrier

Language isn't the only barrier which needs to be overcome when dealing in countries other than our own. Even more important are cultural barriers. Some people, for instance, are from 'low context' cultures such as North America, Britain, Sweden, Switzerland and Germany. They are people who spell things out verbally, while people from high context cultures like France, Japan, Spain, Greece, Saudi Arabia, China and South Korea, communicate by nuance and implication and are less dependent on the spoken word.

If you are talking to people from a low context culture they will lay their cards on the table, while someone from a high context background may leave the most important things unsaid.

In the Orient it is seen as challenging to look someone too directly in the eye, and in Japan it is also difficult to read the reactions of people you are talking to as they will smile, nod and make polite noises which are designed to encourage the speaker to continue. This is often misinterpreted by Westerners as agreement. Japanese executives can also be seen sitting in meetings with their eyes closed. To a Westerner this seems discourteous, but the elimination of visual inputs allows them to listen more acutely.

There is also a range of gestures which would pass unnoticed in some countries, but which could be the gravest of insults in others. It is always wise to consult a native of the culture that will predominate in any audience, if you are at all unsure of the rules.

KEY POINTS

- Language barriers can be climbed
- Be yourself – even when abroad
- Be aware of the culture barriers

· 28 ·

Visual Aids

Sometimes Kingstree clients get the impression that we are against using visual aids. That is not the case.

We are not against the use of visual aids, as long as they are genuinely contributing to what presenters are saying by re-inforcing the messages.

The vast majority of people, however, use too many aids. The result is that at best the graphics fail to contribute, and at worst they can even act as distractions.

Far too much highly-priced management talent is wasted narrating slide shows.

Visual aids – slides, flip charts, videos, computer-generated graphics, hand-outs or anything else which the audience is invited to observe – can enhance a presentation if used properly. They can help an audience to remember key points, and they can support and reinforce what you have already said. Unfortunately, too few presenters know how to use visual aids effectively.

The hidden danger in these support items is their power to distract by pulling audience attention away from the presenter.

A visual stimulus will always override what is being said, particularly if it is on a bright screen while the speaker is thrown into relative darkness. The eyes will always be drawn to the screen.

Stopping the audience creating their own pictures

A visual aid can actually prevent an audience from creating their own emotionally powerful, mental illustrations, as we discussed earlier in the book.

If, for instance, I am talking about 747 jets, and I ask my audience to picture a 'jumbo jet', some of them will have a picture of the plane in flight above their homes, while others will picture a plane they saw on a Singapore Airlines advertisement the night before, and others might picture several 747s in British markings parked at Heathrow's Terminal Four.

Whatever the picture evoked in the minds of the listeners, it is vivid and clear in their minds because it is from their own mental library of images.

If, on the other hand, I put a picture of a 747 up on a screen behind me, people may be looking to see which airline owns it, or whether it is the latest model from Boeing, or wondering what the man with the spanner is doing under the wing. And whatever they focus on may set them thinking about something completely different from the message I am trying to put across verbally.

There is rarely any justification for putting a slide up on the screen and talking at the same time. The audience will be reading the slide and not listening to you.

Don't compete with your visual aids

If you want to illustrate a point with a slide, make the point, then put it up and stay silent to allow the audience time to take in the information. When you are ready to talk again cover the screen up or switch to a blank slide, otherwise you have to compete for their attention and their eyes will always win out against their ears.

The best visual aids are the ones which illustrate your points visually, like bar graphs, trend lines, pie charts or photographs. These are simple, straightforward ways to illustrate either complex aspects or vital points of a presentation.

In our view, presenters should never short circuit their messages by letting visual aids steal the show. Anything that distracts the audience from seeing or hearing the presenter is negative.

Some presenters will even try to lead their listeners through a written aid, line by line. Since most audience members can read, this is a complete waste of time because the audience could read it to themselves faster than they can take in what the speaker is saying. So the speaker's words interrupt the flow of their reading and destroy the point of the visual aid because the audience are ahead of the words being spoken.

Ideally, presenters should make a statement, then lead into a visual aid by saying something like '. . . as you can see here . . .', 'let me show you what I mean . . .' or 'here's a picture of what I'm talking about.' They then put it on the screen and scan it with the audience, silently. It might then be all right to make an explanatory remark or two if necessary. After the audience has observed the aid for a few seconds, the presenter should remove it, re-establish eye contact and continue.

If the aids are not removed, the audience's attention will stay focused on them. Presenters should keep their comments to a minimum whenever an aid has the audience's attention. Visual aids and presenters should work with, and not against, each other.

Hand-outs can be the worst

Of all visual aids, hand-outs can most easily divert the audience's attention from the presenter. Ideally, they should be distributed only at the end of a presentation. Their proper function is to summarize the presentation's major points, or to go into more detail than the presenter wants to for fear of clouding the key messages.

When listeners have hand-outs in front of them as a presenter is talking, there is no guarantee they are listening. Data-packed hand-outs provide an alluring alternative to listening. Obviously, in certain cases there is no alternative to distributing a hand-out, then talking the listener through the material. But this approach should only be used when there is no other option. To work effectively, the hand-out should be introduced before it is displayed, so that the listener is clear about what is about to be shown and specifically what he should be looking for.

A leading investment company asked us to work with their sales and

GOOD VISUAL AIDS

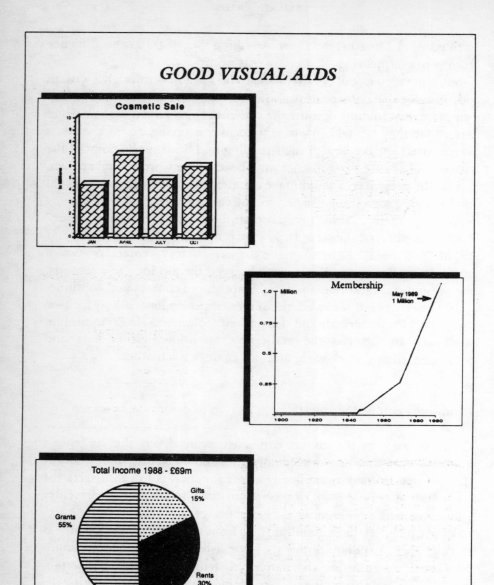

Figure 5

POOR VISUAL AIDS

Global Careers Ltd

W hy are we special

Size and back-up

Management Company and
Lease structuring

Our Approach

Pension Schemes.

Training Programmes

Parking and Transportation

"MILLIONS OF FIGURES"

12	35	56	58	45	26	56	69	52	87	45	85	78
86	98	52	13	4	19	57	49	16	35	24	86	57
91	36	58	48	71	29	35	64	85	94	56	23	75
12	35	56	58	45	26	56	69	52	87	45	85	78
86	98	52	13	4	19	57	49	16	35	24	86	57
91	36	58	48	71	29	35	64	85	94	56	23	75
12	35	56	58	45	26	56	69	52	87	45	85	78
86	98	52	13	4	19	57	49	16	35	24	86	57
91	36	58	48	71	29	35	64	85	94	56	23	75
12	35	56	58	45	26	56	69	52	87	45	85	78
86	98	52	13	4	19	57	49	16	35	24	86	57

Figure 6

new business team, improving the way they present the company to prospective buyers.

Like many others in the industry they used a 'work book', which they would give to the prospect at the beginning of the meeting, and would then go through it step by step.

The moment the presenter opened the book, however, the prospect was starting to read, and had often got to the bottom of the page while the presenter was still talking about the information at the top. Then, worse still, the prospect would turn over the pages to see what else was there.

The result was a complete distraction from what the presenters were saying. It was actually working against them.

Ideally the way they should have been doing it was by using the book as notes for the presenter, and then giving it to the prospect at the end as an aide-memoire to take away. If there were any graphs or illustrations which might be useful to give to the prospect during the presentation, then they should be printed up on a separate card or sheet, to be used when required just like a slide.

Some types of slides are equally counter-productive, however you use them. Slides with a lot of words on them are not good because, as we have said, the audience can read faster than you can read it out to them. Presenters who recognize this problem try to solve it by paraphrasing what is on the slide. This is worse, because it is even more distracting.

Heading slides (the ones that say things like 'Agenda', or 'why we are here', or just carry a company logo) are pointless and distracting to the overall message. If they are forced upon you by a conference organizer, insist that they are taken off the screen the moment you start talking.

It is true that a picture is worth a thousand words, but avoid using visual aids which are just pictures of a thousand words.

The job of an effective presenter is to orchestrate a persuasive blend of information and impressions, with spoken communication at the centre. Visual aids should therefore seek to reinforce something the presenter has said, not be a substitute for the spoken word.

Guarding against conformity

A major American steel company used to take the board of directors away twice a year, including the non-executives, to spend a few days talking about what was going on in the company. That included a series of presentations in the mornings, with discussions and recreation in the afternoons.

Somebody in corporate design came up with the idea of theming the presentations with colours so, for instance, for capital budgets all the background would be green, for profit and loss items the background would be blue and so on. On these backgrounds all the formats for all the slides were to be designed to be completely identical and consistent.

If was a perfectly logical approach, but the outcome was that by the end of the second presentation everything was becoming blurred in the audience's memories. Everything was so similar they couldn't differentiate between them, nor could they distinguish in their minds what the key points were, which meant they couldn't retain them.

This was an example of a sound, logical approach frustrating the effectiveness of the communication.

The dangers of autocue

The autocue machine, or tele-prompter as it is known in America, was invented to create the impression on audiences that the speakers were not reading their material, when in fact they were reading it verbatim. Its first use was in television news broadcasts.

Initially it worked because audiences assumed that the clear glass screens that the messages were projected onto were part of the security systems, making it harder for an assassin to shoot the political leaders who pioneered their use with live audiences.

Once it became widely known that it was a reading device, the autocue began to create a distraction. To start with, the people who knew the screens' true purpose were busy explaining the system to others in the audience, instead of listening to the speakers.

Secondly, the people who use autocues typically have two screens which they refer to, and they go back and forth between them, which means they appear to be looking at the audience the whole time. Although their heads are sweeping back and forth, they have what seems like total eye contact, a situation which bears no relation to how we talk normally, where eye contact is actually infrequent.

So they are creating a distorted view of themselves compared with how they converse normally, and, because they are reading verbatim, they are in danger of using the literary style of language and delivery which we have been working so hard to avoid.

Also, while the speaker appears to be looking at the audience he is really looking at his text and therefore finds it difficult to pick up any reaction he may be provoking in his listeners.

A final problem is that training in their use is necessary. Many senior executives ask for prompters at a conference on the assumption that they can simply speak, after perhaps one run-through, with no further preparation. This may occasionally be true but can lead to disastrous –if amusing – consequences. A Kingstree client with no practice stood up at a conference and began to read his text from the two clear screens. After a moderate start he began to pick up speed: as the teleprompt operator heard him going faster she began to scroll the text faster through the machine. Each began to race the other, the speaker finally accelerating until he sounded almost like Donald Duck and the audience burst into gales of laughter!

The system falls down completely if speakers are doing something like an eight-line quote, because the autocue makes it look as if they have remembered it by heart, and the audience is going to find such a feat of memory hard to believe, and therefore distracting.

The professional broadcasters and news anchor-men who use autocue all the time realize the dangers. As a result they are disciplined to look away from the camera every so often, usually to glance down at their notes, which restores the impression that they are talking spontaneously, and breaks the eye contact which would otherwise be unwavering and disconcerting for the viewer.

KEY POINTS

- Visual aids must contribute not distract
- Only use them to illustrate your points visually
- Never compete with visual aids
- The eye always takes precedence over the ear
- Control what your audience sees
- Allow audiences to create their own mind pictures
- Keep hand-outs to the end
- Never use headings or topic slides
- Too much conformity of image can confuse more than it clarifies
- Beware of the autocue/tele-prompter

Summary

Clearly it is impossible to write a book which will provide all the guidance required to learn to play golf, fly a plane or learn to make effective presentations. The key to acquiring any skill is to understand conceptually what one is trying to do, then work at building one's ability and confidence gradually through constant practise.

One of the problems with traditional advice on spoken communications is that it establishes a rigid set of criteria for how one should behave when making a presentation. The underlying premise is that describing recent events to the shareholders informing the board about a new strategy or convincing employees to support a 'quality initiative' through large presentations, somehow requires behaviour which is different for and specific to these occasions.

Since few of us actually address hundreds of colleagues, or face tough questions from the press or investment analysts on a weekly basis, each presentation becomes a special event. So, under the traditional rules calling for 'presentation behaviour', we only really get to pratice a few times a year.

The approach laid out in *High Impact Business Presentations* allows for constant daily practise and reinforcement, because it builds on those communication skills which are an integral part of one's personal conversational style, evolved and developed over many years.

What we have tried to do in this book is to reveal the critical elements of normal conversational communication which allow people to transmit and receive information effortlessly when they are relaxed and operating in a low stress environment. We have also pointed out how an increase in stress leads to distortion in a presenter's perception of how fast the clock is moving and contributes to a change in his or her behaviour.

Our experience with thousands of clients confirms that the key to effective presentation is to maintain one's own innate conversational style, no matter how great the increase in stress. This allows our clients and readers of this book to practise their presentation techniques every single day, when they are participating in formal or informal meetings, talking to customers or colleagues on the telephone, or discussing the rare discovery of a messy room with a teenage son or daughter!

The point is that we all need to recognize what we are doing when we 'get it right' and achieve any successful communication, and then stay with it. Don't allow yourself to adopt some foreign 'presentation persona' that conforms to an arbitrary set of standards which are hard to remember and which make you uncomfortable. Be yourself, confident that you now understand what that really means. And practise. There is no substitute for practise in becoming a more effective communicator.

When we meet clients who are innately shy, we never suggest that they should try to change their personality. That would be absurd. What we tell our clients is that they can greatly increase their confidence in making those vital presentations by seeking opportunities to address a luncheon of the Rotary Club or Chamber of Commerce, to speak up at meetings of their golf or tennis club, where they will have a chance to validate the approach we have described in this book, in presentations where the risk is low.

Once people discover that they can aproach the most daunting presentation in exactly the same way as they approach informal communication their apprehension dwindles and their confidence soars.

All of us in the The Kingstree Group are fortunate to have the opportunity to work with hundreds of successful executives, professionals from all disciplines, and political leaders. In many cases we are advising clients who have years of experience of making successful presentations before they meet us. But whether the clients are seasoned veterans, or young bankers or accountants who are nominated to join a major new business pitch for the first time, they find our advice universally reassuring. Being confident that they can 'be themselves' allows them to direct their concentration toward the message, to read their listeners' reactions, and to stop worrying about how they are performing.

Our objective in writing *High Impact Business Presentations* is to help our readers to understand the basic principles which will allow them to communicate more effectively in virtually all business and social situations. We have laid out those key principles so that they are easy to understand and adopt. We have tried to keep it simple. And there is no 'secret ingredient' that we have left out of the recipe for success.

The Chinese character for 'crisis' combines the characters for 'danger' and 'opportunity'. I know that there are very senior people in business and politics who still look at a major speech as a sort of crisis. I hope that by following our advice they can eliminate the danger and look at any presentation they might have to make as representing a real opportunity.

I would like to close by inviting you to try the various approaches we have set out, by encouraging you to be bold in taking on communication challenges as they come along, and above all to have fun doing it.

Index